The Big
Bear Cub
Scout Book

MY BEAR
TRAIL
BEGINS
HERE

Brian Ackerman
MY NAME

8   283
MY DEN NUMBER   **MY PACK NUMBER**

_____
MY DEN LEADER'S NAME

_____
MY DEN LEADER'S TELEPHONE NUMBER

_____
MY DEN CHIEF'S NAME   **HIS TROOP NUMBER**

_____
DATE I RECEIVED MY BEAR BADGE

1

Contents

Illustrations of Baloo by Robert Depew

Copyright 1984
BOY SCOUTS OF AMERICA • IRVING, TEXAS
NO. 3228 Printed in U.S.A. 500M585
ISBN 0-8395-3228-8

The Big Bear Trail (Achievements)

Arrow Point Trail (Electives)   152-247

Welcome to the BEAR TRAIL

Read the next few pages in your new Cub Scout book. Find out how Baloo helped Mowgli learn the Law of the Pack.

HOW BALOO TAUGHT MOWGLI THE LAW OF THE PACK

Long ago in the jungles of India, a small brown boy was separated from his family when his village was raided by the fierce tiger, Shere Kahn. He was found and protected by a family of wolves who lived in the jungle. They named him Mowgli and asked Akela, the leader, if he could join their pack. The pack council met once a month at full moon. Akela asked, "Who speaks for this cub?" Baloo, the wise old brown bear, the only other creature allowed at the pack council because he taught the wolf cubs the law of the pack, stood up on his hind paws and said, "I speak for the man cub. I will teach him."

Bagheera, the black panther, slipped into the council ring and said, "I, too, speak for the man cub." Shere Kahn snarled in rage. This is how Mowgli came to live with the wolf family in the jungle and learned the ways of a wolf cub.

INTRODUCTION

As Mowgli grew older, Baloo taught him the law of the pack and the secret, master words that let him talk to the other jungle creatures, all except the Bandar-log, the monkey people who did not obey the law of the pack. They decided to make their own law, and thought it would be a fine idea to capture Mowgli and make him their leader. They were so thoughtless and silly the other animals paid no attention to them.

The Bandar-log grabbed Mowgli one day while he was taking a nap. They carried him high above the trees to a deserted city where none of the other jungle creatures lived. While he was being carried through the branches, Mowgli called for help. Rann, a hawk, heard him call and flew swiftly to tell Baloo and Bagheera.

Baloo the bear and Bagheera the panther were furious with rage and grief. They could not follow through the tree tops, but set out through the jungle to rescue Mowgli. Baloo knew that the Bandar-log's greatest fear was of Kaa, the snake. "He can climb as well as they can. Let us go to Kaa."

"What can he do?" asked Bagheera. "He is not of our tribe, and has most evil eyes."

"He is old and cunning. Above all, he is always hungry," said Baloo hopefully.

Kaa agreed to help and all three started for Monkey City. They reached the abandoned city by nightfall. Baloo and Bagheera moved in first. The Bandar-log swarmed over them, biting and scratching, for the monkey people are brave only when the odds are in their favor. Things were going badly for Baloo and Bagheera when Kaa arrived. Baloo was right; the Bandar-log were terribly frightened of Kaa. They climbed the walls and towers of the city trying to get as far away as possible. Kaa battered down the cage where the Bandar-log had put Mowgli and set him free.

Kaa began weaving in his hunger dance, making all who watched—the Bandar-log, Baloo, and Bagheera—helpless to move. Mowgli shook his friends who were falling under Kaa's spell and woke them just in time. The three made their escape back to their own part of the jungle.

Mowgli had learned to live as a wolf cub and had begun to learn the wisdom of the bear, but he needed older friends to teach him things that would protect him. Like Mowgli, you can call on parents and leaders to help you.

WHAT EVERY PARENT SHOULD KNOW

Rudyard Kipling wrote this story about Mowgli in *The Jungle Book*. Baden-Powell, the founder of Scouting, loved a good story and decided to make Mowgli's story the basis of his Wolf Cub program in England. He believed that basic truths can best be taught through stories.

Your Cub Scout is older and it is time that Baloo, the serious bear who knows the master words of the jungle, takes over. This is your new role.

As you begin to play the part, remember this quotation from Baden-Powell: "Our standard for badge earning is not the attainment of a certain level of quality of knowledge or skill, but the amount of effort the boy put into acquiring such knowledge or skill." As you work with your boy, Baden-Powell reminds you to: "Discriminate where to be generous and where to tighten up."

You can let Baloo help you do this by telling your Cub Scout: "Baloo knows you can do better than that," or "Let's see if Baloo can help." If you let him, Baloo can become an imaginary friend and adviser to you both. Baloo can help you become better acquainted with your Cub Scout.

There will be good times and not-so-good times when chattering playmates try to coax your Cub Scout into mischief. When that happens, remind him of the Bandar-log, the monkey people who got Mowgli into trouble. Baloo despised the monkey people because he respected the law of the pack. Just as their careless ways led the Bandar-log to be Kaa's dinner, boys who behave like them may be swallowed by laziness, boredom, and drugs.

The best way to prevent this is to become a good friend of your boy and his playmates. Working through this book with your Cub Scout is a practical way to build his defense while enjoying the family fun of Cub Scouting.

Bobcat Trail

If you were a Wolf last year, you will remember "The Story of Akela and Mowgli." If this is your first year as a Cub Scout, Baloo hopes you liked his story.

When you join the Cub Scouts, no matter how old you are you become a Bobcat first.

1. Learn the CUB SCOUT PROMISE.
   "I, ... , promise to do my best to do my duty to God and my country, to help other people, and to obey the Law of the Pack."

EXPLAINING THE PROMISE

Promise. . . To promise means you will keep your word when you tell someone you will do something. People will trust you when you keep your promises.

Do my best. . . We are not all alike, so when we do our best it means that we have tried as hard as we can.

Do my duty. . . We know what is right and what is wrong; so we know what we should do at all times. When we do our duty to God, this means we practice our religion at home and at our place of worship.

When we do our duty to our country, we stand up for our country. Be proud you are an American. Stand up for your rights and the rights of all Americans.

To help other people...Do things for people even when you are not asked. Be good to people, help them and don't expect to be rewarded.

2. Learn the LAW of the PACK.

"The Cub Scout follows Akela. The Cub Scout helps the pack go. The pack helps the Cub Scout grow. The Cub Scout gives goodwill."

Remember Akela (Ah-kay'-lah) in the story. Akela is a Cub Scout name for a good leader. This can be your father, mother, uncle, grandparent, teacher, den leader, Cubmaster, or den chief. Cub Scouts learn to be good leaders. To be a good leader you must also learn to follow good leaders and learn from them.

To help the pack go...You should go to den meetings and pack meetings, help your den in work and play. Help your pack in goodwill efforts and money-earning projects.

Helps the Cub Scout grow...The pack gives you a chance to learn new skills and to meet new friends. The pack gives you a chance to be proud of yourself when you earn each new rank.

Gives goodwill...A Cub Scout is kind and thinks about making other people happy.

CUB SCOUT SIGN. Make this sign with your right hand. Hold your arm up straight. Do not bend your elbow.

The two fingers stand for the two points of the promise; to help other people and to obey. In Indian sign language this means *wisdom*. When you say the Cub Scout Promise or the Law of the Pack, give the Cub Scout sign.

THE HANDSHAKE. When you shake hands, use your right hand. Put the first two fingers along the inside of your friend's wrist. This means that you are brothers in Cub Scouting and that both of you help other people and obey the Law of the Pack.

THE SALUTE. The Cub Scout salute means you respect our country's flag or the leader you are saluting. Salute with your right hand. If you are wearing your Cub Scout cap, place your two fingers on the brim. If you do not have on a cap, place your two fingers over your eyebrow.

THE MOTTO. "Do Your Best." This means to try as hard as you can in everything you do.

WHAT DOES *WEBELOS* MEAN? Webelos (We'-buh-lows) has a secret meaning for Cub Scouts— *We'll Be Loyal Scouts. Loyal* means that you will keep your Cub Scout Promise.

NOW YOU CAN BECOME A BOBCAT CUB SCOUT.

Your Den, Pack, and Uniform

A group of Cub Scouts, called a **den**, usually meets once a week in the den leader's home. The dens all get together once a month for a pack meeting. Remember, as a Bear Cub Scout, you are a member of a pack. Remember, too, the Law of the Pack: "The Cub Scout helps the pack go." You should bring adult members of your family with you to each pack meeting. You will not only be proud to have them there to see you and your friends having fun but to take part in the ceremony when you have earned an award. The award is given to an adult member of your family, and he or she will in turn give it to you in front of the whole pack. This is a way of saying "thank you" to your family for their help in earning your award.

Now that you are a second-year Cub Scout, you have a blue neckerchief to wear with your Cub Scout uniform. Don't forget your cap; it is fun to wear! If you don't wear your uniform to den and pack meetings, and on outings

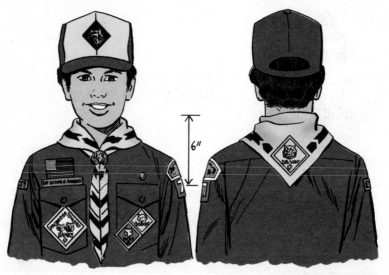

BOBCAT TRAIL

and special events, no one will be able to tell that you are a Cub Scout, and that you have earned all the emblems sewed on your uniform shirt. Be proud to wear the Cub Scout uniform. Did you know there are Cub Scouts all around the world? You are a member of a large group of boys your age.

There are service stars, temporary emblems, Summertime Pack Award pins, Honor Unit emblems, recruiter emblems, and lots of other emblems you can earn and wear on your uniform. (Ask your den leader to help you earn them and show you where each is worn.)

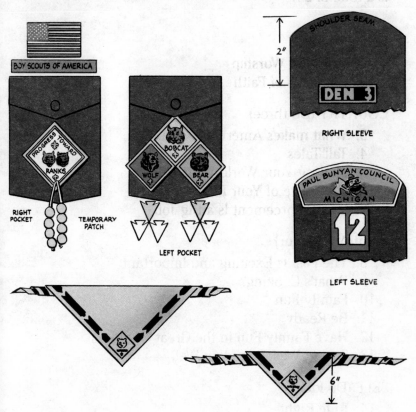

The Big BEAR Trail

You must complete 12 achievements to be a Bear Cub Scout. You can pick the ones you want to do from four different groups. You have a wide choice because there is a total of 24.

GOD (Do one)
1. Ways We Worship
2. Emblems of Faith

COUNTRY (Do three)
3. What makes America Special?
4. Tall Tales
5. Sharing Your World With Wildlife
6. Take Care of Your Planet
7. Law Enforcement Is a Big Job

FAMILY (Do four)
8. The Past Is Exciting and Important
9. What's Cooking?
10. Family Fun
11. Be Ready
12. Have Family Fun in the Great Outdoors
13. Saving Well, Spending Well

SELF (Do four)
14. Ride Right

15. Games, Games, Games!
16. Building Muscles
17. Information, Please
18. Jot It Down
19. Shavings and Chips
20. Sawdust and Nails
21. Build a Model
22. Tying It All Up
23. Sports, Sports, Sports
24. Be a Leader

When you finish an achievement, you will need to have an adult member of your family sign and date your book. You will then take your book to the next den meeting and your den leader will record it on the Cub Scout (Den) Advancement Chart and initial your book.

When you have done all 12 Bear achievements, you become a Bear Cub Scout. You will get your Bear badge from an adult member of your family at the pack meeting. You may count any extra achievement requirements you earn as arrow point credits. Have them signed and dated.

THE BIG BEAR TRAIL

Ways we worship

W e are lucky. The people who wrote and signed our Constitution were very wise. They understood the need of Americans to worship God as they choose. A member of your family will be able to talk with you about your duty to God. Remember, this achievement is part of your Cub Scout Promise:

"I, _____, promise to do my best to do my duty to God and my country...."

REQUIREMENT

Practice your religion as you are taught in your home, church, synagogue, mosque, or other religious community.

I worship God:

in song

in prayer

in study

and by kind and thoughtful acts toward others

CUB SCOUT LEADER BALOO SAYS: When you have done this requirement, have a parent or an adult sign here.

____/_____

____ Bear credit
Date and signature for
____ Arrow point credit

2 ACHIEVEMENT
Emblems of faith

Many signs remind us of God. Among them are a 6-pointed star, a cross, and a crescent. There are many other religious symbols. One of them may appear on a special emblem you may earn to wear on your uniform.

Learn more about your faith from your rabbi, minister, priest, imam, or elder.

REQUIREMENT

Earn the religious emblem of your faith.

PARVULI DEI for Cub Scouts who are Roman Catholic, or Eastern Rite Catholic.

CHI RHO for Cub Scouts who are Eastern Orthodox.

METTA for Cub Scouts who are Buddhist.

GOD AND FAMILY for Cub Scouts who are Episcopalian.

GOD AND FAMILY for Cub Scouts who are Protestants.

GOD AND FAMILY
for Cub Scouts who
are Lutheran.

ALEPH for Cub
Scouts who are
Jewish.

Do one achievement for your GOD

FAITH IN GOD for Cub Scouts who are
members of the Church of Jesus Christ of
Latter-day Saints.

The LIGHT OF THE WORLD for
Cub Scouts who are members of
the Reorganized Church of Jesus
Christ of Latter Day Saints.

SILVER CREST for
Cub Scouts of the
Salvation Army.

The Cub Scout who has earned the religious emblem of his faith may wear the Religious Emblem Square Knot, No. 5014, on his uniform, above the left pocket.

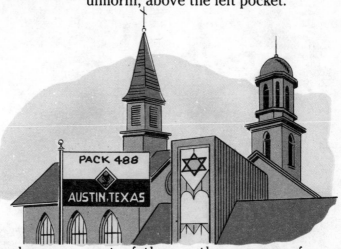

Many packs are a part of the youth program of churches, mosques, and synagogues. If your pack is a part of a church, mosque, synagogue, or other religious community, try to do Good Turns for it. Remember, a Cub Scout gives goodwill.

CUB SCOUT LEADER BALOO SAYS: When you have done this requirement, have a parent or an adult sign here.

_____/ _____ Date and signature for
achievement 2
— OR —
_____/ _____ Date and signature for
arrow point credit

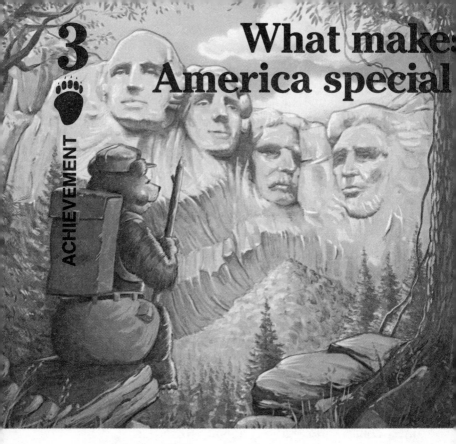

What make: America special

A mericans believe everyone should be free and should control his or her own life. We have the right to own property and to worship any way we want. Our laws protect each of us equally.

People did not always live this way. How men and women got together and started our free way of life makes an interesting story.

The story is still being written. Probably your parents and grandparents and even your great-grandparents are a part of it. You can be part of it, too.

As a Cub Scout, you can be one of the reasons that America is special. Help others. Be a good citizen. Take part in the life of your country.

REQUIREMENTS

Do requirement *a* and three of the following requirements:

a. Write or tell what makes America special to you.

America, the beautiful, is special because of her:

Opportunities

People

Freedom

____ Bear credit
____/_____ Date and signature for
____ Arrow point credit

b. With the help of your family or den leader, find out about two Americans. Tell the things they did or are doing to improve our way of life.

Look for great Americans in:

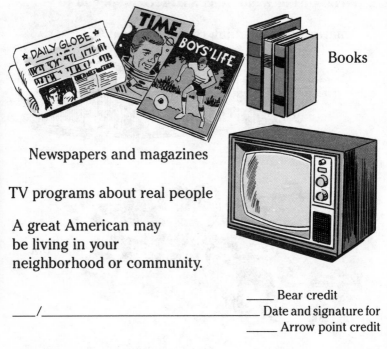

Books

Newspapers and magazines

TV programs about real people

A great American may
be living in your
neighborhood or community.

____ Bear credit
____/_____ Date and signature for
____ Arrow point credit

c. Find out something about the old homes near the place where you live. Go and see two of them.

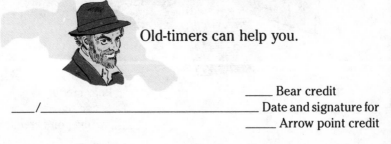

Old-timers can help you.

____ Bear credit
____/_____ Date and signature for
____ Arrow point credit

Do three achievements for your COUNTRY

d. Find out where places of historical interest in or near your town are located. Go and visit one of them with your family or den.

These might be battlefields, monuments, buildings, or a place where a famous story or poem was written.

_____ Bear credit

____/_____ Date and signature for

_____ Arrow point credit

e. Pick your favorite state or home state. Name its state bird, tree, and flower. Describe its flag. Give the date it was admitted to the union.

Use an encyclopedia to get this information:

State bird_____

State tree_____

State flower_____

Date admitted to the union_____

My sketch of the
state flag

_____ Bear credit

____/_____ Date and signature for

_____ Arrow point credit

f. Be a member of the color guard in a flag ceremony for your den or pack.

A color guard usually has four Cub Scouts. Numbers 1 and 4 are the guards. Number 2 carries the U.S. flag. Number 3 carries the den or pack flag.

_____ Bear credit

____/_____ Date and signature for

_____ Arrow point credit

g. Display the U.S. flag in your home or fly it on three national holidays.

Memorial Day, last Monday in May
Honors these who died
in defense of our country.

Flag Day, June 14
Marks the day in 1777 when
Congress adopted the Stars
and Stripes
as our flag.

Independence Day, July 4
Celebrates the adoption of the
Declaration of Independence
from Great Britain.

Labor Day, first Monday in September
Honors all work-
ing men and women.

Veterans Day, November 11
Honors the living veterans of
all our wars. It is the anni-
versary of the end of World
War I in 1918.

_____ Bear credit
____/_____ Date and signature for
_____ Arrow point credit

CUB SCOUT LEADER BALOO
SAYS: When you have done
requirement *a* and three others,
have a parent or an adult sign
here.

____/_____ Date and signature for achievement 3

Tall tales

A modern-day tall tale might be a fisherman's story about "the big one that got away." What we mean by "tall tales" in the Bear book are stories, customs, songs, and sayings from our American past. These were handed down by families or groups of people. They tell us about the life and spirit of our forefathers. American folklore is told in stories and songs, some true and some told to make the story better. One thing you can count on about tall tales or folklore is they tell about the happiness, fears, dreams, and hopes of early Americans. American folklore is full of wonderful people and adventures.

REQUIREMENTS

Do all three requirements.

a. Tell in your own words what folklore is. List some folklore stories, folksongs, or historical legends from your own state or part of the country.

SASQUATCH or BIGFOOT. A giant manlike creature of the Pacific northwest. Huge footprints and fleeting glimpses are all that anyone has seen of him.

PONY EXPRESS RIDERS. Between 1860 and 1861, riders carried the mail from Missouri to California. They rode at a gallop for 2000 miles, changing horses about every 10 miles.

PAUL BUNYAN and BABE THE BLUE OX. A tall-tales lumberman who leveled a forest in one swing of his ax. Then trimmed the trees and stacked the logs for Babe, who swooshed them out of the woods in one haul.

PECOS BILL. A tall-tales cowboy who was raised by coyotes. Fought a 10-foot rattlesnake, tamed it, and used it as a whip. Caught and rode a mountain lion like a horse. Staked out New Mexico and dug the Grand Canyon.

RIP VAN WINKLE. The hero of Washington Irving's story of a hen-pecked husband who went into the mountains to hunt. There he found a group of little men playing nine pins. He joined them and after the game lay down to take a nap which lasted 20 years.

HIAWATHA. The main character of Longfellow's poem about an Indian chief:
"You shall hear how Hiawatha
Prayed and fasted in the forest,
Not for triumphs in the battle,
And renown among the warriors,
But for profit of the people
For advantage of the nations."

CHARLIE PARKHURST. A stage-coach driver before there were railroads. Charlie was unusual, because Charlie was a lady.

THE LOST DUTCHMAN. A mine, not a man, that is still lost. Somewhere in the Superstition Mountains of Arizona there is a hole in the ground loaded with gold.

JOHNNY APPLESEED. Jonathan Chapman, his real name (1775-1847), Christian missionary who planted orchards in the wilderness. He was a friend of the Indians and the settlers. During the War of 1812 he saved the settlers from a surprise attack.

DANIEL BOONE. Hunter and trailmaker who led settlers over the Allegheny mountains into Kentucky. Some say he was half man, half horse, and half alligator.

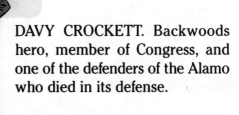

DAVY CROCKETT. Backwoods hero, member of Congress, and one of the defenders of the Alamo who died in its defense.

JOHN HENRY. A steel-driving champion whose record has never been equaled. In 35 minutes John Henry drove two 7-foot shafts into solid rock while a steam drill made only one 9-foot shaft.

Do three achievements for your COUNTRY

ZORRO. A hero who lived on his father's hacienda in southern California when it was a colony of Mexico ruled by a governor who taxed and oppressed the people. Hiding his identity behind the mask of Zorro, Don Diego would ride to protect the cruel governor's victims.

EL DORADO. The Indians told the Spaniards that somewhere in the West was a fabulous city of gold.

BARBARA FRIETCHE. Took up the flag the men hauled down and defied Stonewall Jackson. "Shoot, if you must, this old gray head, but spare your country's flag," she said. A poem by John Greenleaf Whittier.

OLD STORMALONG. A tall-tales sailor who grew tired of the sea and said he was going to put his oar on his shoulder and walk west until someone asked: "What's that funny looking stick on your shoulder?" There he vowed to settle down.

ICHABOD CRANE. An awkward schoolmaster in Washington Irving's "The Legend of Sleepy Hollow," who was scared out of town on Halloween night by the ghostly headless horseman (who was not really a ghost, but a jealous rival dressed as the horseman).

MOLLY BROWN. A tough frontier lady from the Colorado silver mining town of Leadville, who helped save some of the survivors of the Titanic.

KING KAMEHAMEHA. For 28 years, the ruler of Hawaii long before Hawaii was a part of the United States. He began to rule in 1782 and died in 1810.

CASEY JONES. A famous engineer who stayed with his train to warn others of the crash. He died with one hand on the whistle and one hand on the brake. Old 638 crashed into the freight train that had not cleared the siding.

FOLKLORE MATCH GAME

1. Sasquatch or Bigfoot
2. Pony Express Riders
3. Paul Bunyan and Babe
4. Pecos Bill
5. Johnny Appleseed

6. Daniel Boone

7. Davy Crockett
8. John Henry
9. Zorro
10. El Dorado
11. Barbara Frietche

12. Old Stormalong

13. Molly Brown
14. Ichabod Crane
15. Rip Van Winkle

16. Hiawatha
17. Charlie Parkhurst

18. Lost Dutchman
19. King Kamehameha

20. Casey Jones

___ Was of royal blood
_15_ Slept a long time
_4_ Cracked a whip

_6_ Bravest of all
_14_ Knocked off his horse by a pumpkin
_10_ Built with a precious metal
___ Died in the Alamo
_13_ She was unsinkable
___ Got tired of the sea
___ Beat a machine
___ Robbed the rich; gave to the poor
___ Warned settlers of an attack
___ Is famous in Kentucky
___ Keeps out of sight
___ Could not have built houses without them
___ Rode a strange horse
___ Wasn't interested in glory
_20_ Stayed with his train
_1_ Isn't a man, but a something
_2_ Carried the mail

_____ Bear credit
____/_____ Date and signature for
_____ Arrow point credit

b. **Name at least five stories about American folk-lore. Point out on a United States map where they took place.**

_____ Bear credit
____/_____ Date and signature for
_____ Arrow point credit

c. **Read two folklore stories and tell your favorite one to your den.**
Den leader initial_____

_____ Bear credit
____/_____ Date and signature for
_____ Arrow point credit

CUB SCOUT LEADER BALOO SAYS: When you have done all three requirements, have a parent or an adult sign here.

____/_____ Date and signature for achievement 4

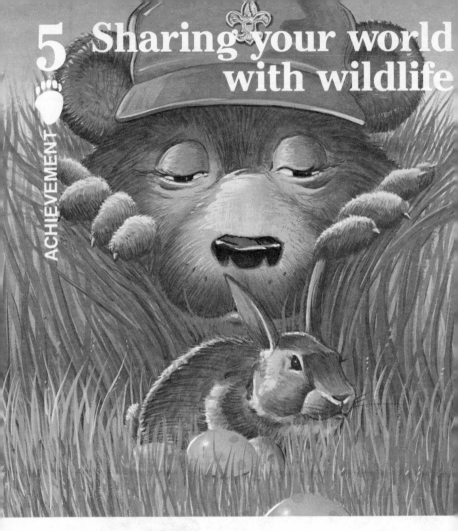

5 Sharing your world with wildlife

Every living creature has a place in this world, and there is room for all of us. Birds, fish, and animals need clean water, food, and air just as Cub Scouts do.

You can help protect wildlife by following the fishing and hunting laws. Keep wildlife areas beautiful. Pick up trash along the trails, streams, and lakeshores. Put it in rubbish barrels where it belongs.

REQUIREMENTS

Do four of the following requirements.

a. Choose a bird or animal that you like and find out how it lives. Make a poster showing what you have learned.

Get to know birds or animals by:

Watching them

Reading about them

_____ Bear credit
_____/_____ Date and signature for
_____ Arrow point credit

b. Build or make a bird feeder or bird house.

WINDOW FEEDER. Use water-proof plywood or wide 1-inch wood. Nail a lip all around to hold in the food. Cut two braces to hold up the outer edge. Screw braces to tray and house.

BIRDHOUSES. Birds that nest in the hollows of trees will nest in birdhouses. Six of the more common ones are bluebird, chickadee, titmouse, nuthatch, wren, and house finch.

Do three achievements for your COUNTRY

BIRDHOUSE SIZES

BIRD	FLOOR	DEPTH	HOLE ABOVE FLOOR	HOLE SIZE	PLACE ABOVE GROUND
Bluebird	5x5 in.	8 in.	6 in.	1½ in.	5-10 ft.
Chickadee	4x4 in.	8-10 in.	6-8 in.	1½ in.	6-15 ft.
Titmouse	4x4 in.	8-10 in.	6-8 in.	1¼ in.	6-15 ft.
Nuthatch	4x4 in.	8-10 in.	6-8 in.	1¼ in.	12-20 ft.
Wren	4x4 in.	6-8 in.	4-6 in.	1-1¼ in.	6-10 ft.
House Finch	6x6 in.	6 in.	4 in.	2 in.	8-12 ft.

_____ Bear credit

____/_____ Date and signature for

_____ Arrow point credit

c. Explain what a wildlife conservation officer does.

Get to know a conservation officer from your state or federal fish and wildlife service. Look in your phone book. Tell the officer that you are a Cub Scout and are working on this achievement. The person you talk with may be one or more of these three things:

RESEARCHER. Studies the lives and habits of wild animals and birds. Finds out how wild things live, where they live, what they eat, what eats them, how they raise babies, and how they survive during the winter.

MANAGER. Helps provide wild animals with things they need—food, water, shelter, and living space.

EDUCATOR. Writes articles for newspapers about wildlife. He or she may be on radio or TV shows, make movies, or give talks to Cub Scout packs or school classes on wildlife.

_____ Bear credit

___/_____ Date and signature for
_____ Arrow point credit

d. Visit one of the following:

___ Zoo   ___ Wildlife refuge

___ Nature center   ___ Game preserve

Ask a conservation officer if any of these places are near your home. Plan to take a trip to one of them with your family or den.

Do three achievements for your COUNTRY

___ Bear credit

___ / _____ Date and signature for

___ Arrow point credit

e. Name one animal that has become extinct in the last 100 years. Tell why animals become extinct.

Talk with a conservation officer or librarian.

___/_____ Date and signature for achievement 5.

CUB SCOUT LEADER BALOO SAYS: When you have done four requirements, have a parent or an adult sign here.

___/_____ Date and signature for achievement 5.

Take care of your planet

The Earth is your planet. That means you have to help take care of it. It's the only planet we will ever have. Conserve energy. Save our resources. Plant trees and flowers.

REQUIREMENTS

Do three of the following requirements:

a. Save 5 pounds of glass or aluminum, or 1 month of newspapers, and turn them in at a recycling center.

Separate your trash at home.

Stack and tie newspapers.

Rinse and dry bottles and aluminum cans.
To save space, crush aluminum cans.

_____ Bear credit

_____ /_____ Date and signature for
_____ Arrow point credit

b. Plant a tree in your yard, or on the grounds of the group that operates your Cub Scout pack, or in a park. Be sure to get permission first.

Trees make buildings more attractive and cooler in summer.

PLANTING SEEDLINGS

1. Push spade into the ground and push the handle up straight.

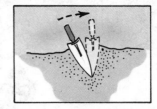

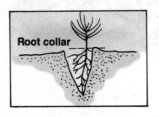

2. Remove the spade and place the seedling with its root collar at ground level.

3. Push spade into the ground 2 inches from the seedling. Push the handle away from the plant. This will firm the soil at the bottom of the roots.

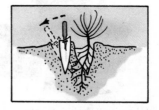

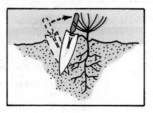

4. Now pull the handle toward the plant to firm the soil at the top of the roots.

5. Fill in the spade hole by scraping the soil with your shoe.

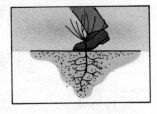

6. Pack the soil firmly around the seedling with your foot.

Some seedlings will be taller than you are in 5 years. You will be able to sit in their shade in 10 years.

____ Bear credit
____/_____ Date and signature for
____ Arrow point credit

c. **Call city or county officials or your trash hauling company and find out what happens to your trash after it is hauled away.**

Is any of it:
• Recycled?
• Burned to generate electricity?

If it is dumped and buried in a land fill, what will happen to the land afterward?

____ Bear credit
____/_____ Date and signature for
____ Arrow point credit

d. **Do a water-usage survey in your home. Note all the ways water is used. Look for any dripping faucets.**

___ Cooking   ___ Garden
___ Dishwashing ___ Shrubs and trees
___ Laundry   ___ Swimming pool
___ Showers and baths ___ Drinking
___ Toilet   ___ Fountains
___ Lawn   ___ Hobbies

HOW TO REPAIR A LEAKY FAUCET

1. Turn off the water. You will find a shutoff valve under the sink.

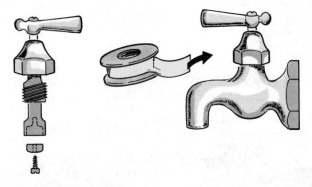

2. Protect the finish of the packing nut by wrapping it with adhesive tape.
3. Loosen the packing nut carefully. Turn and lift out the stem assembly.
4. Remove the screw at the bottom of the stem assembly. Pry out the old washer. Clean out the place where it was.
5. Replace the worn washer with one that fits. Insert flat side down. Replace the screw.

6. Wipe the valve seat clean. Replace the stem assembly. Carefully tighten the packing nut. Before removing the adhesive tape, turn on the valve. Test the faucet.

_____ Bear credit

____ / _____ Date and signature for

_____ Arrow point credit

e. Discuss with one of your parents the ways your family uses energy.

___ Solar   ___ Diesel fuel
___ Natural gas ___ Electricity
___ Propane   ___ Wood
___ Gasoline   ___ Kerosene
___ Heating oil ___ Charcoal briquettes

_____ Bear credit

____ / _____ Date and signature for

_____ Arrow point credit

f. Find out more about your family's use of electricity.

Visit or call your power company for help in completing this requirement. Ask how electricity is made for your home.

Check off the appliances you have and underline the ones that use a lot of electricity.

___ Toaster	___ Air conditioner
___ Stove	___ Fans
___ Microwave	___ Water heater
___ Refrigerator	___ Dishwasher
___ Heater	___ Washing machine
___ Radios	___ Clothes dryer
___ TV	___ Hair dryer
___ Clocks	___ Iron
___ _____	___ _____
(Other)	(Other)

To save electricity:

- Turn off lights when no one is using them.

- Turn off the TV when no one is watching.

Winter

- Turn the thermostat to 68° in winter and 78° in summer.

Summer

____ Bear credit

___/_____ Date and signature for
____ Arrow point credit

CUB SCOUT LEADER BALOO SAYS: When you have done three of these requirements, have one of your parents or an adult sign here.

___/_____ Date and signature for achievement 6.

ACHIEVEMENT 6   51

Law enforcement is a big job!

Police officers need our help as they work to protect us. We need to understand ways of taking care of ourselves. Crime has always been a problem everywhere. But we can do something about it. This achievement will help you understand how the police and others fight crime. It will also show you ways that you can help.

REQUIREMENTS

Do four of the following requirements:

a. Make a set of your own fingerprints.

. R. THUMB	2. R. INDEX	3. R. MIDDLE	4. R. RING	5. R. LITTLE
. L. THUMB	7. L. INDEX	8. L. MIDDLE	9.L. RING	10. L. LITTLE

Use an ink pad. Press an inked finger on a piece of paper. When you can get a good sharp print, make your set of prints right here in the book. Those prints are your signature. No one else on Earth has prints just like them.

Police look for fingerprints at the scene of a crime so that when they arrest someone, they can check that person's prints with the ones found at the scene of the crime. If the prints match, it proves that the person has been at the crime scene.

_____ Bear credit
____/_____ Date and signature for
_____ Arrow point credit

b. Make a plaster cast of a shoeprint in the mud.

Make a good clear track in sand or soft earth. Put a cardboard ring around it. Mix water with plaster of paris until it's like thin pudding. Pour it over the track and let it harden.

Pick up the hardened plaster. Clean off any of the dirt that has stuck to it. Take off the shoe that made the track. Compare it with the plaster shoe.

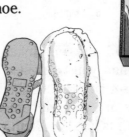

Police do this to find evidence that would tie a suspect to a crime scene. If they can match a shoeprint at the crime with a suspect's shoe, that would be an important piece of evidence.

_____ Bear credit

____/_____ Date and signature for

_____ Arrow point credit

c. Check the doors and windows of your home.

Be sure you have tight, strong locks on your doors and windows. Do this with one of your parents.

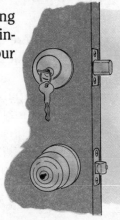

Deadbolt should be over 1 inch long

____ Bear credit
____/_____ Date and signature for
____ Arrow point credit

d. Visit your local sheriff's office or police station.

Meet the deputy sheriff or the police officer who patrols your neighborhood.

____ Bear credit
____/_____ Date and signature for
____ Arrow point credit

e. Be sure you know where to get help in your neighborhood.

Is there a:
- Block Home?
- Emergency Home?
- Helping Hand Home?
- Family Friend?

_____ Bear credit

___/_____ Date and signature for

_____ Arrow point credit

f. Be sure fire and police numbers are listed by the phone at your home.

Police _____

Fire _____

 Memorize these numbers. Without lifting the receiver, dial or punch these numbers in the right order. See if you can do it with your eyes closed.

Check the inside cover of your phone book for emergency numbers.

_____ Bear credit

___/_____ Date and signature for

_____ Arrow point credit

g. Know what you can do to help law enforcement.

If you see a crime being committed or some dangerous activity, tell your parents or call the police.

Get the facts:
- What's happening?
- Where is it happening?
- Who is doing it?
    Can you describe the person?
    Did you get the license number?

WARNING

OPERATION I.D.
THIS PROPERTY PROTECTED

_____ Bear credit
____/_____ Date and signature for
_____ Arrow point credit

CUB SCOUT LEADER BALOO SAYS: When you have done four of these requirements, have a parent or an adult sign here.

____/_____ Date and signature for achievement 7.

8 The past is exciting and important

ACHIEVEMENT

The Times DATE 1981

FIRST SPACE SHUTTLE LAUNCHED TODAY!

Something that took place 100 years ago can seem as exciting and interesting as something that took place yesterday.

You learn about America's past in school. Your family has a history, too; so has your community, and your Cub Scout pack.

REQUIREMENTS

Do three of the following requirements:

a. Visit your library or newspaper office. Ask to see back issues of newspapers.

What were the headlines on:

- The day you were born?

_____

_____

_____

- July 21, 1969?

_____

_____

_____

- The day you were 5 years old?

_____

_____

_____

_____ Bear credit

____/_____ Date and signature for

_____ Arrow point credit

b. Find someone who was a Cub Scout a long time ago. Talk with him about what Cub Scouting was like then.

What did they do at:

- Den meetings?

  _____

  _____

  _____

- Pack meetings?

  _____

  _____

  _____

- What kind of uniform did they wear?

  _____

  _____

  _____

_____ Bear credit

____/_____ Date and signature for

_____ Arrow point credit

c. Start a pack scrapbook and give something to it.

You might give a:
- Picture
- Pack meeting program in which you took part
- Newspaper from your school
- Report on a Good Turn or service project done by your den or pack

____ Bear credit

____/_____ Date and signature for
____ Arrow point credit

d. Trace your family back through your grand-parents or great grandparents; or, talk to your grandparents about what it was like when they were younger.

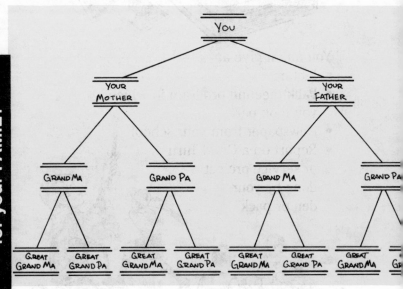

What did your grandparents do:

- At school?
- During holidays?
- At home to help around the house?

_____ Bear credit

_____/_____ Date and signature for

_____ Arrow point credit

e. Find out some history about your community.

Perhaps you can talk to someone who has lived in your community for a long time. How did people heat their homes?

- Where was the first school?
- Where was the firehouse?
- Where were the places of worship?

You may find some books about the history of your community in your library.

____ Bear credit
____/_____ Date and signature for
____ Arrow point credit

f. Keep a diary for 2 weeks.

Jot down some of the things you do each day. Be sure to save your diary. When you grow up, you'll have some history about yourself.

____ Bear credit
____/_____ Date and signature for
____ Arrow point credit

CUB SCOUT LEADER BALOO SAYS: When you have done three requirements, have a parent or an adult sign here.

____/_____ Date and signature for achievement 8.

9 What's cooking

W e all like to eat good things. Good things seem to taste even better when we make them ourselves. In this achievement you will want to work with someone who knows how to cook. You and that person can cook up some great food.

DO NOT TRY TO DO ANY OF THESE REQUIREMENTS UNLESS AN ADULT IS HELPING YOU.

REQUIREMENTS

Do four of the following requirements:

a. Bake cookies.

HOW TO MAKE OATMEAL COOKIES

Preheat oven to 350° F.

¾ cup vegetable shortening	1 teaspoon vanilla
	3 cups uncooked oats
1 cup firmly packed brown sugar	1 cup all-purpose flour
	1 teaspoon salt
½ cup granulated sugar	(optional)
1 egg	½ teaspoon baking
¼ cup water	soda

Beat together shortening, sugars, egg, water, and vanilla until creamy. Add combined remaining ingredients; mix well. Drop by rounded teaspoonfuls onto a greased cookie sheet. Bake at 350° F. for 12 to 15 minutes. For variety, add chopped nuts, raisins, chocolate chips, or coconut. Makes about 60 cookies.

If you don't like oatmeal cookies, use another recipe from a cookbook. Or use a packaged mix, but follow directions on the package.

____ Bear credit

___/_____ Date and signature for

____ Arrow point credit

b. If your parent or guardian says it is all right, volunteer to make snacks for the next den meeting.

HARD-BOILED EGGS. Place eggs in a cooking pot or pan. Cover with cold water. Bring the water to a full boil. Reduce the heat and simmer for 15 minutes. Remove from the stove and drain the hot water and replace it with cold. Drain and let dry. The egg is perfectly packaged by nature for picnics.

CARROT AND CELERY STICKS. Brush carrots and celery clean. Trim off dark spots. Cut off tops and bottoms. Cut in half lengthwise. Cut the half strips in quarters. Then cut into sticks.

POPCORN. Pour in enough cooking oil to cover the bottom of the pan. Add corn, spreading it over the bottom so that each kernel is touching bottom. Place pan on medium-high burner. Gently shake the pan so that the kernels do not burn. When the kernels begin to pop, cover the pan with a tight-fitting lid. Continue to shake the pan until the corn stops popping. Remove from the heat. Pour in a bowl. Add melted butter or margarine. Salt to taste.

_____ Bear credit
____/_____ Date and signature for
_____ Arrow point credit

c. Prepare one part of your breakfast, one part of your lunch, and one part of your supper.

JUICE. Squeeze fresh oranges, or you can use frozen orange juice or a mix. Follow the directions on the can or the package.

COOKED CEREAL. Follow directions on the package.

SANDWICHES AND SOUP. This combination makes a good lunch any time of the year. Use canned soup or a mix. Follow the directions on the can or package. Make your sandwiches with whatever you have. Luncheon meat, cheese slices, sliced tomatoes, and lettuce with mayonnaise makes a super sandwich. You don't need to have all that in one sandwich. You could make three different kinds. Peanut butter and jelly also makes a good sandwich. Spread peanut butter on one slice of bread and jelly on the other. Put the two together and slice in half. Replace the covers, clean the spreading knife.

Requirement 9c continued ➡

BOILED POTATOES. Use a potato peeler to peel enough potatoes for your family. (One for each person is about right.) Wash the potatoes and cut in quarters. Put ½-inch of water in a pan with the potatoes. Add ¼-teaspoon of salt. Cover the pan. Bring the water to a boil, then reduce the heat. Cook for 20 minutes or until you can push a fork into a potato easily. Remove from the heat. Drain the water, using the cover to keep the potatoes from spilling out. Replace on the heat for about 10 seconds to dry and fluff the potatoes. Serve with butter or margarine or gravy.

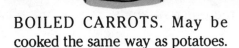

BOILED CARROTS. May be cooked the same way as potatoes.

SPAGHETTI. Follow the directions on the package.

_____ Bear credit

_____/_____ Date and signature for

_____ Arrow point credit

d. Make a list of the "junk" foods you eat. Discuss "junk" food with your parent or teacher.

Junk foods have too many calories and too few nutrients. Foods with a lot of sugar may not have the vitamins and minerals you need.

- Soft drinks
- Candy
- Ice cream
- Chips

____/_____ Teacher's initials

____ Bear credit

____/_____ Date and signature for

____ Arrow point credit

e. Make some healthful after-school snacks or some snacks for watching television.

NUTS AND BOLTS. Mix peanuts and raisins together with some dry cereal.

_____ Bear credit

_____/_____ Date and signature for

_____ Arrow point credit

f. Make a dessert for your family.

INSTANT PUDDING. Empty the contents of the package into a bowl. Follow directions on package.

BROWNIES. Follow directions on the package.

GELATIN. Follow directions on the package.

_____ Bear credit
_____/_____ Date and signature for
_____ Arrow point credit

CUB SCOUT LEADER BALOO SAYS: When you have done four requirements, have a parent or an adult sign here.

_____/_____ Date and signature for achievement 9.

10 Family fun

Families live together and take care of each other. Get to know your family better by spending more time with them.

Plan a trip or a fun evening together. Talk about your plans. A parent or guardian is like Baloo, a Cub Scout leader, who can show you many useful and interesting things.

REQUIREMENTS

Do both of these requirements:
a. Go on a trip with members of your family.

VISIT ONE OF THE FOLLOWING:
___ Park   ___ Museum
___ Airport   ___ Seashore
___ Farm/Ranch

BEFORE YOU GO. Think of the things that you may need and pack them in a handy bag. Your needs will be different if you are going by car, train, bus, subway, ferry, bicycle, or on foot.

CAR BEHAVIOR AND SAFETY. An adult family member should check the car for safe operation before the trip begins.

You will be expected to get yourself ready and agree to:

• Buckle yourself in with a seatbelt or safety strap. Suggest others use theirs. Make sure infants ride in safe car seats or child restraints.
• Change seats only at roadside stops. No climbing from one seat to another while the car is moving.
• Keep hands and arms inside the car.
• Keep doors locked at all times.
• Keep the rear window of a station wagon closed.
• Save paper and trash for roadside barrels. Don't litter.
• Pack everything in the trunk or carrier except snacks, game bag, and books.
• Don't be noisy or shout inside the car.

- Use good manners and be considerate of others while traveling on a bus, train, subway, or ferry.

WHAT TO DO FOR A TRIP IN TOWN. Call and make an appointment. Arrive on time. Stay with your group. Treat your guide with respect. Listen to what he or she says. Keep the noise down —be polite.

_____ Bear credit
_____/_____ Date and signature for
_____ Arrow point credit

b. Have a "family-make-and-do-night."

Get together and make homemade games, things for the holidays, or party decorations.

STADIUM SEAT. Place rug or foam rubber scraps between two pieces of carpeting. Lay the rope handle in place, cement, and sew around the edges.

Do four achievements for your FAMILY

BOOT JACK. Make it easy to take off your boots or overshoes. Any piece of 1-inch scrap wood that is a foot long and 3 inches wide will do. Cut a V in one end. Then nail a short piece of wood beneath the point of the V.

BULLETIN BOARD. A long narrow family bulletin board is easy for all to read. Put the grownups' notices at the top and the children's at the bottom. Use a panel from a corrugated box. Cover it with plain cloth. Tack it to a narrow wooden frame.

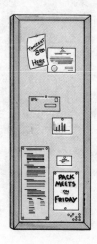

_____ Bear credit
____/_____ Date and signature for
_____ Arrow point credit

CUB SCOUT LEADER BALOO SAYS: When you have completed both requirements, have a parent or an adult sign here.

____/_____ Date and signature for achievement 10.

11 Be ready!

You expect fire fighters, police, and paramedics to protect you in an emergency. Sometimes, though, you have to take care of yourself or someone else until help arrives. You should be ready to do the right thing if this happens.

Fires and accidents can be frightening, and it is natural to be scared. That is why we think about what to do before an emergency happens.

In a very serious case, there is little time to stop and figure out what to do. That is why we must be ready. If someone's clothes are on fire, or breathing has stopped, you must act at once. In other cases there may be time to stop a few seconds and think about what to do.

Your best way to handle most cases is to get help from an adult. If you are not with an adult, go outside and try to stop a passing car. **Do not** stand in the road or street. Most drivers will stop if you wave to them and they see your Cub Scout uniform.

A good way to be ready is to carry enough change for a pay telephone. In some places you can dial 911 for help. Find out if you can do that where you live.

REQUIREMENTS

Do the first four requirements; the last one is recommended, but not required.

a. **Tell what to do in case of accident in the home. Parent needs help. Clothes catch on fire.**

What should you do if you are at home with your mother or father and he or she falls downstairs and gets hurt? Talk it over with your parent and think about this:

(1) Be calm and make your parent as comfortable as possible without moving him or her. DO NOT TRY TO MOVE AN INJURED PERSON. You will make the injury worse if you do.

(2) GET HELP! If there is someone in the yard or nearby, send that person to call a neighbor or telephone an ambulance. Do it yourself, if no one else is around.

a. Continued

    (3) Stay with your parent. Use a blanket to keep him or her warm.

What should you do if someone's clothes catch on fire? Find out. Talk it over with your parents or teacher.

    (1) Usually a person panics and starts to run — STOP HIM! Running fans the flames and makes them spread.

    (2) If the person can be caught, force him to the ground or floor. Roll the victim over and over to smother the flames. Wrap with a rug, blanket, or sweater working from the neck down. If you can't catch him, yell "STOP! STOP! STOP!" Throw yourself on the ground and roll, so he'll do what you do. **Cover your face.**

    (3) As soon as you can, help the person get to a place where the burned parts of the body can be covered with clean dressings and treated by a doctor.

What should you do if your own clothes catch on fire?

(1) STOP where you are. DO NOT RUN!

(2) Drop to the floor or ground.

(3) Roll and cover your face.

(4) If indoors, grab a rug, blanket, or a coat and wrap yourself as you roll. Start at the neck.

What should you do if your house catches on fire?

(1) First, get everyone out of the house!

(2) Don't try to put the fire out yourself, unless it is a very small fire.

(3) Call the fire department from a neighbor's house.
(4) When the fire department arrives, let them know everyone is out of the house.

_____ Bear credit

____/_____ Date and signature for

_____ Arrow point credit

b. Tell what to do in case of a water accident.

A boat overturns and you are in it, what do you do?
(1) DON'T PANIC. Grab the boat and stay with it.
(2) Help the other passengers to find a place where they can hold on. NO ONE SHOULD TRY TO SWIM ASHORE. Stay with the boat, it will support you. Wait for rescuers.

(3) If the boat can be turned right side up, get inside and sit or lie as low as possible on the bottom.

Someone slips off a bank into the water, what do you do?

(1) Reach him, if possible, with your hand or leg. Take off your sweater or shirt and toss an end to the person. You can also extend a stick, fishing pole, branch, or anything that is handy.

(2) Throw something to him that will float:
  • A cushion, inner tube, plank, etc.
  • A ring buoy, if available.

Someone falls through the ice, what do you do?
(1) Remember, if you get too close, you might break through, too.
(2) Find something to throw to the person.
(3) Use something to reach like a ladder, a long branch, or anything that he can grab. Then you can pull him out.

(4) When he is out of the water, get him someplace warm.

_____ Bear credit
____/_____ Date and signature for
_____ Arrow point credit

c. Tell what to do in case of a school bus accident.
   (1) Always know where emergency exits are whenever you get on a bus.

   (2) In case of an accident, follow directions of the driver. If the driver is injured, keep calm—tell others to take it easy and get out of the bus by the emergency exits. Move to the side of the road, away from traffic.
   (3) Help the bus driver get everyone out without pushing.

_____ Bear credit
____/_____ Date and signature for
_____ Arrow point credit

d. Tell what to do in case of a car accident.
   (1) Be calm. Help the adults by doing what you are told.
   (2) Suggest to the driver that the car be left where it is until the police come. Ask an adult to direct traffic around it.

(3) Don't go out into the road yourself. Watch for other cars. All passengers should get out of the car on the side away from traffic.

(4) DON'T MOVE ANYONE WHO IS BADLY INJURED.

____ Bear credit
____ / _____ Date and signature for
____ Arrow point credit

e. Have a health checkup by a physician (optional).

RECOMMENDED BUT NOT REQUIRED. A health checkup is a good thing to have each year. It will show you what to do for your health's sake.

____ Bear credit
____ / _____ Date and signature for
____ Arrow point credit

CUB SCOUT LEADER BALOO SAYS: When you have done the first four requirements—the last requirement is recommended, but not required—have a parent or an adult sign here.

____ / _____ Date and signature for achievement 11.

ACHIEVEMENT 11

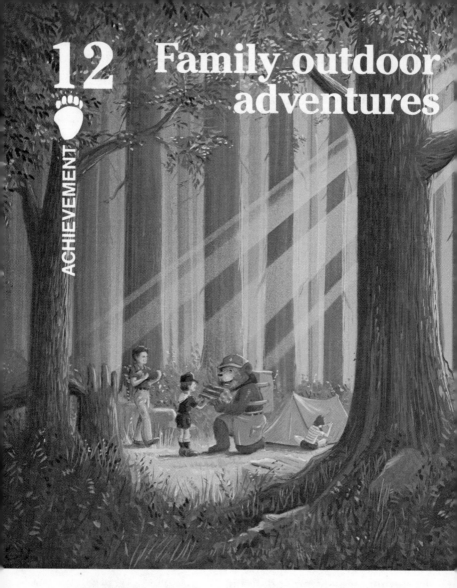

12 Family outdoor adventures

ACHIEVEMENT

You may live in a state with snow in winter, or you may live where it is warm all the time. No matter where you live, being outside and doing things with your family is great. You can have fun together and get to know one another better.

REQUIREMENTS

Do three of the following requirements:

a. Go camping with your family.

CAMPING. When you live outdoors overnight in a tent, camper, trailer, or motorhome, that's camping. Be sure to help your family pack for the trip. You will need to be ready for changes in weather. Nights are cold and sudden rainstorms are possible. Pack those things that keep you warm and dry.

____ Bear credit

____/_____ Date and signature for

____ Arrow point credit

b. Go on a hike with your family.

HIKING. A hike is more than a walk. When you hike, you go exploring to find out something. You can hike in the city, forest preserves, county or state or national parks, or even the zoo.

KEEPING DRY. When you are far from shelter, what will you do when it rains? Some smart outdoor families have solved that

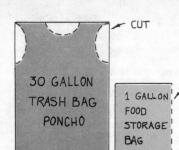

30 GALLON
TRASH BAG
PONCHO

CUT

1 GALLON
FOOD
STORAGE
BAG
RAIN HAT

CUT

problem. Each family member carries a plastic trash bag poncho. When it rains, just slip it over your head and wear it like a sleeveless sweater. You can also make a rain cap from a plastic food storage bag.

Do four achievements for your FAMILY

Keep away from hilltops and trees that may draw lightning.

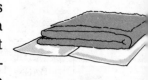

DON'T GET LOST! Stay with your family. Don't wander off by yourself. Carry a police whistle to signal for help if you get lost. Three sharp blasts on your whistle means EMERGENCY!

LEAVE YOUR TRACKS. When hikers are lost, searchers need to know what the lost hiker's tracks look like. Before you leave on a hike into the woods, fold a soft towel in half. Spread it on a newspaper and cover the towel with a piece of aluminum foil. Wearing your hiking shoes, stand on

the aluminum foil and step off. The print you make can help searchers find you. Write the color of your clothes on a slip of paper. Keep it with your footprint.

BEFORE YOU LEAVE. Tell someone where you are going and when you will return. Give that person the aluminum foil tracks of your hiking shoes. If you do not get back on time, that person can tell the authorities that you are missing and how you are dressed.

STAY WHERE YOU ARE. If you think you are lost, sit down and wait in the open where people can see you. Searchers will find you. DON'T TRY TO FIND YOUR WAY BACK.

_____ Bear credit

_____ / _____ Date and signature for

_____ Arrow point credit

c. Have a picnic with your family.

How about a breakfast picnic?

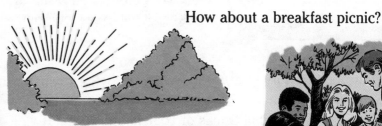

How about an all-star favorite food roundup? That's when everyone brings his or her favorite food to share with others.

____ Bear credit

____/_____ Date and signature for

____ Arrow point credit

d. Attend an outdoor event with your family.

A craft fair

A hot-air balloon race

A bird count

A fish derby

_____ Bear credit
____/_____ Date and signature for
_____ Arrow point credit

e. Plan your outdoor family day.

Think of some things you would like to do outdoors.
Explain these ideas to your family. Listen carefully
to the ideas other family members have.

_____ Bear credit
____/_____ Date and signature for
_____ Arrow point credit

CUB SCOUT LEADER BALOO
SAYS: When you have done three
of these requirements, have a parent or an adult sign here.

____/_____ Date and signature for achievement 12.

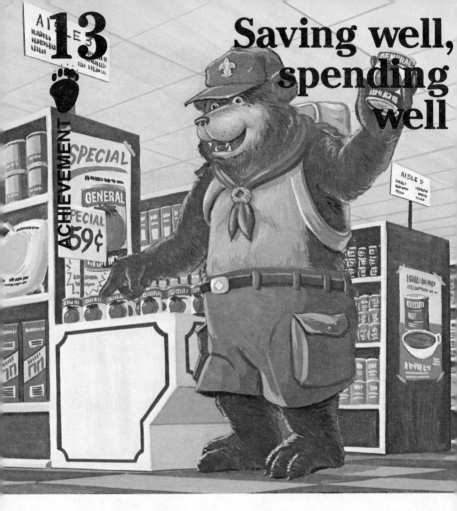

13 Saving well, spending well

People can do a lot of things with money. They can buy or build a house. Cars, clothes, food—almost everything we need or use takes money. We can make some things. We can raise or grow some foods. When we do that we save money.

You may have an allowance, or you may earn money for the things you need each week. Money is going to be important to you all of your life. Now is a good time to learn how to control it.

REQUIREMENTS

Do four of the following requirements:

a. **Go grocery shopping with a parent.**
Compare prices of different brands of the same item. Check the prices at different stores.
Read the ads in your newspaper.

_____ Bear credit
____/_____ Date and signature for
_____ Arrow point credit

b. **Set up a savings account.**

When you put your money in a bank or a savings and loan, you put your money to work. The bank loans your money to people. They pay the bank an extra amount of interest for the use of the money. Then every 3 months or so the bank adds interest to your money. Interest is money you did not have to earn. But, you still have the money in the account to draw out if you really need it.

If you have a savings account you may not easily be tempted to spend your money for things that you do not really need.

_____ Bear credit
____/_____ Date and signature for
_____ Arrow point credit

c. **Keep a record of how you spend money for 2 weeks.**

Date	How I Spent Money	How Much I Spent
_____	_____	_____
_____	_____	_____
_____	_____	_____
_____	_____	_____
_____	_____	_____
_____	_____	_____
_____	_____	_____
_____	_____	_____
_____	_____	_____
_____	_____	_____
_____	_____	_____
_____	_____	_____
_____	_____	_____

When you have finished the record, look over each line. Did you spend that money wisely? Did you buy some things you didn't need? What can you do to spend your money better from now on?

_____ Bear credit
____/_____ Date and signature for
_____ Arrow point credit

d. Make believe you are shopping for a car for your family.

Look through newspaper car ads. Compare the price of cars. Are the cars large enough for your family? How about miles per gallon? Pick one that you think is best for your family. Report your choice to one of your parents. Tell why you picked that car.

_____ Bear credit

____/_____ Date and signature for

_____ Arrow point credit

e. Discuss family finances with one of your parents.

Find out how you can help with family finances.

____ Bear credit

____/_____ Date and signature for

____ Arrow point credit

f. Play a board game with your family that in-volves the use of make-believe money.

Does the person who wins most of the time take fewer chances? Or more? Are you getting better at the game?

____ Bear credit

____/_____ Date and signature for

____ Arrow point credit

g. Figure out how much it costs for each person in your home to eat one meal.

Before the meal is prepared, jot down the cost of each of the foods used.

WHEAT BREAD 45
MILK ½ GAL 42
LETTUCE 72
CELERY 22
TOMATOES 22
ONIONS
BROCCOLI 32
CARROTS 32
ICE CREAM 21
POTATO CHIPS 34

COST PER MEAL

PEOPLE	FOOD COST

Divide the total cost of the food by the number of people who will be eating the meal.

Is this more or less than what it would cost to eat out?

_____/_____
_____ Bear credit
Date and signature for
_____ Arrow point credit

CUB SCOUT LEADER BALOO SAYS: When you have done four of the requirements, have a parent or an adult sign here.

_____/_____ Date and signature for achievement 13.

Bicycle motocross, 10-speeds, bike hikes—there are all kinds of bicycles and things to do with them today. Boys and girls and grownups, too, are riding bikes more and more.

Bicycling is fun, it's good for you, and it's interesting. But bicycling can be dangerous if you are not careful. Be sure you know the safety rules for bicycling, and be sure you and your mom or dad always keep your bike in good shape.

Here are the requirements to complete your Ride Right Achievement.

REQUIREMENTS

Do requirement *a* and three more:

a. **Know the rules for bike safety. If your town requires a bicycle license, be sure to get one.**

RULES FOR BIKE SAFETY

1. Obey all traffic signs and signals.
2. Ride single file on streets and highways and keep to the right.
3. Ride in a straight line—don't do stunts or weave in and out of traffic.
4. Use proper hand signals when in traffic.

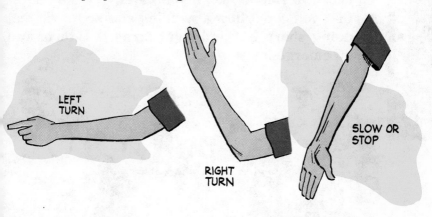

LEFT TURN

RIGHT TURN

SLOW OR STOP

5. Slow down and look carefully before crossing intersections.
6. Be alert for other vehicles, especially for cars pulling out from the curb.
7. Don't shoot out of blind alleys and driveways.
8. Give pedestrians the right-of-way.
9. Don't carry another rider.
10. Don't hitch onto cars and trucks.

a. Continued

11. Be sure your bike has good brakes and a warning bell or horn.
12. If you must ride at night, be sure to have a headlight on the front of your bike and a red glass reflector on the rear.

____/_____
____ Bear credit
Date and signature for
____ Arrow point credit

b. Learn to ride a bike, if you haven't by now. Show that you can follow a winding course for 60 feet doing sharp left and right turns, a U-turn, and an emergency stop.

____/_____
____ Bear credit
Date and signature for
____ Arrow point credit

c. Keep your bike in good shape. Identify the parts of a bike that should be checked often:

____ Brakes   ____ Chain
____ Spokes   ____ Tires
____ Pedals   ____ Reflectors
____ Seat   ____ Lights

Which of these parts should be fixed by an expert repairman only? Explain and show how you protect your bike from bad weather.

Always keep your bike under shelter when it is not in use. If it gets wet from rain or snow, wipe it dry. Keep the moving parts well lubricated. Have someone help you learn how to adjust any parts that need adjusting.

____ Bear credit
____ /_____ Date and signature for
____ Arrow point credit

d. Change a tire on a bicycle.

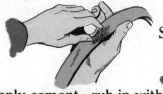

Scrape tube over the hole.

Apply cement—rub in with finger and let dry.

Remove cover from patch.

Apply patch with pressure.

Put a little air in tube. Insert tube in tire and force on rim.

____ Bear credit

____/_____ Date and signature for

____ Arrow point credit

e. Protect your bike from theft. Use a bicycle lock.

Write down your bicycle's serial number. Have your name engraved somewhere on your bike.

____ Bear credit

____/_____ Date and signature for

____ Arrow point credit

Do four achievements for YOURSELF

f. Ride a bike for 1 mile without rest, and be sure to obey all traffic rules.

____ Bear credit
____/_____ Date and signature for
____ Arrow point credit

g. Plan and take a family bike hike.

____ Bear credit
____/_____ Date and signature for
____ Arrow point credit

CUB SCOUT LEADER BALOO SAYS: When you have done requirement *a* and three others, have a parent or an adult sign here.

____/_____ Date and signature for achievement 14.

Games, games, games!

Let's play a game! Everybody likes games, especially outdoor games. Here are some game ideas. You may have played some of them, but you will probably find new ones. Games are fun and they teach you how to think before you act.

REQUIREMENTS

Do two of the following requirements:

a. Set up the equipment and play any two of these outdoor games with your family or friends.

____ Backyard golf	____ Kickball
____ Badminton	____ Tenpins
____ Croquet	____ Tetherball
____ Sidewalk	____ Horseshoes
shuffleboard	____ Volleyball

____ Bear credit

____/_____ Date and signature for

____ Arrow point credit

b. Play two organized games with your den.

Pick games that everyone can play.

_____

_____

____ Bear credit

____/_____ Date and signature for

____ Arrow point credit

c. Select a game your den has never played. Explain the rules. Tell them how it is played, then play it with them.

Did they understand your explanation?

Do you think they will want to play it again?

____ Bear credit

____/_____ Date and signature for

____ Arrow point credit

CUB SCOUT LEADER BALOO SAYS: When you have done two requirements, have a parent or an adult sign here.

____/_____ Date and signature for achievement 15.

16 Building muscles

Games, stunts, and contests with other Cub Scouts help you become physically fit and alert. Den and pack activities are aimed at keeping you healthy.

This achievement will develop your speed, balance, and reactions. The more you practice, the stronger you will become. A strong body is important to you now, and it will be even more important to you as you grow older.

REQUIREMENTS

Do all of the following requirements:

a. Do physical fitness stretching exercises. Then do sit-ups, push-ups, the standing long jump, and softball throw.

Stretching exercises

Sit-ups

Standing long jump

Push-ups

Softball throw

____ Bear credit

____/_____ Date and signature for

____ Arrow point credit

b. With a friend, compete in at least six different two-person contests.

____ ONE MAN PUSH OVER LINE. Face your opponent. Grasp his shoulders. On the word "Go" try to push him across the line. Your goal line is 10 feet in front of you; your opponent's is 10 feet behind you. Only pushing is permitted.

____ CHINESE PULL. Stand back to back, lean forward, place your hands on the floor. Now grab your opponent's right hand between your legs. On the signal "Go" try to pull your friend out of his half of a circle.

____ ONE MAN PULL OVER LINE. Face your friend 3 feet apart. Grasp his wrists and try to pull him across the goal line 10 feet behind you. Only pulling is allowed.

THE BIG BEAR TRAIL • SELF

____FOOT PUSH. Sit facing your friend. Have the soles of your feet touching with your knees bent. Try to push your friend out of a circle or over a line. Feet must always be touching feet. Push on the floor with your hands.

____ONE-LEGGED HAND WRESTLE. Raise your left ankle with your left hand. Take your friend's right hand. On the word "Go" try to upset him. You win if he lets go of his foot or loses his balance.

____STAND UP BACK-TO-BACK PUSH. Stand back to back with your elbows linked. Try to push your friend across a line 10 feet away. Only pushing is allowed.

____BACK-TO-BACK PUSH. Sit back to back. Fold your arms across your chest. Using your feet on the floor, try to push your friend over a line. Don't push or butt with your head!

b. Continued

____ HAND WRESTLE. Grasp your friend's right hand. Stand with your feet braced against each other—right foot to right foot. Spread your feet so that you are well balanced. On the signal "Go" try to throw your friend off balance. First to move a foot or touch the ground with a hand is the loser.

____ ELBOW WRESTLE: Lie on your stomach, facing your friend. Place your right elbow on the floor and clasp your friend's hand. Try to force his hand to the floor at the command "Go." Elbows must not leave the floor. Try it with left hands.

____ Bear credit

____/_____ Date and signature for
____ Arrow point credit

c. Compete with your den or pack in the crab relay, gorilla relay, 30-yard dash, and kangaroo relay.

_____ Bear credit
____/_____ Date and signature for
_____ Arrow point credit

NOTE TO PARENTS. If a licensed physician certifies that the Cub Scout's physical condition for an indeterminable time doesn't permit him to do three of the requirements in this achievement, the Cubmaster and the pack committee may authorize substitution of any three of the arrow points in the elective section of this book.

CUB SCOUT LEADER BALOO SAYS: When you have done three of the requirements, have a parent or an adult sign here.

____/_____ Date and signature for achievement 16.

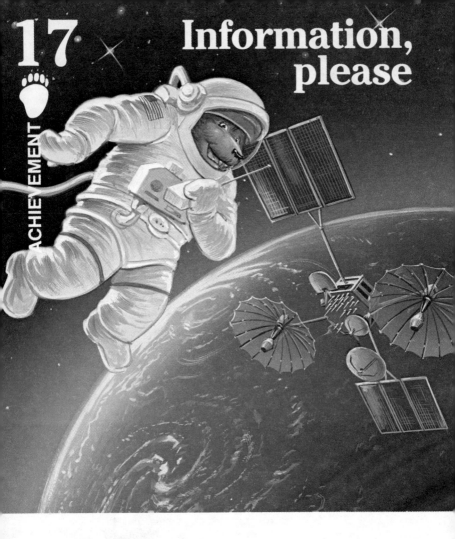

17

ACHIEVEMENT

Information, please

Information is a big word with a simple meaning. It means facts, and telling someone a fact is communication. We can also get information from newspapers, books, magazines, radio, TV, and computers.

As you complete this achievement, you might be surprised to find out all the ways we can give and get information.

REQUIREMENTS

Do requirement *a* and three more of the following requirements:

a. With an adult in your family, select a TV show. Watch it together.

After the show, talk about it. What did you like?
- What did you learn?
- What didn't you like about it?
- What would you have changed?

_____ Bear credit

___/_____ Date and signature for

_____ Arrow point credit

b. Visit a newspaper office, or TV or radio station and talk to a news reporter.

- Where does the reporter get the news?
- How does the reporter put the story together?
- Where does the story go after the reporter finishes it?

_____ Bear credit

___/_____ Date and signature for

_____ Arrow point credit

c. Play a game of charades at your den meeting, or with your family at home.

Charades is a guessing game. Each part of a word is acted out. Suppose the word was "football." You might point to your foot. When your side yells "foot," you could pretend to kick a ball. During this game don't use your voice at all.

d. Visit a place where computers are used.

Talk to the person in charge. Find out how they put information into the computer.

What does the computer do with the information?

How do the people get information from the computer?

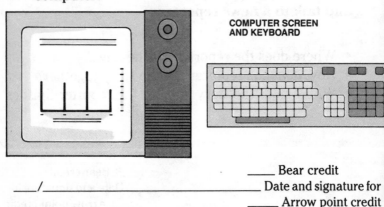

COMPUTER SCREEN AND KEYBOARD

(Side tab: Do four achievements for YOURSELF)

e. Write a letter to a company that makes something you use.

C.K. JORDAN
353 KATHERINE
DALLAS, TX. 76429-0412

CRAFT, INC.
APRIL DRIVE 1-83
FT. WORTH, TX 75328-1311

Tell them what you think about their product.

Ask them where it is made.

____ Bear credit
____ / _____ Date and signature for
____ Arrow point credit

f. Talk with one of your parents or another family member about how getting and giving facts fits into his or her job.

How do they get the facts they need?
- Does someone tell them directly, or over the phone?
- Do they read it on paper, or books, or computer screen?
- What do they do with the facts?
- Do they pass the facts along to others?

____ Bear credit
____ / _____ Date and signature for
____ Arrow point credit

CUB SCOUT LEADER BALOO SAYS: When you have done requirement *a* and three others, have a parent or an adult sign here.

____ / _____ Date and signature for achievement 17.

18

Jot it down

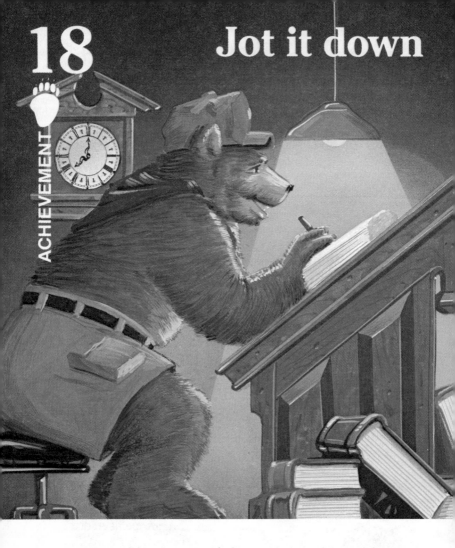

Writing is one of the most important things man has learned to do. Writing lets us send messages to far away places, make a lasting record of things we want to remember, and read what others have done or thought in the past. Being able to write clearly is a useful and satisfying skill. Do this achievement to learn more about it.

REQUIREMENTS

Do five of the following requirements:

a. Make a list of the things you want to do today. Check them off when you have done them.

Before you go to bed, make a list of the things you should do tomorrow. Put the list on the bulletin board or some place where you will see it often so you won't forget anything.

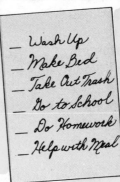

_____ Wash Up
_____ Make Bed
_____ Take Out Trash
_____ Go to School
_____ Do Homework
_____ Help with Meal

_____ Bear credit
____ / _____ Date and signature for
_____ Arrow point credit

b. Write two letters to relatives.

Dear Grandpa
Last night I won the Pinewood Derby with my race car.
Thanks for helping me with it.

Tell them what you have been doing in Cub Scouting.

_____ Bear credit
____ / _____ Date and signature for
_____ Arrow point credit

c. Keep a daily record of your activities for 2 weeks.

Time yourself. When do you: TIME

Get up in the morning?   _____
Eat breakfast?   _____
Go to school?   _____
Eat lunch?   _____
Get home from school?   _____
Eat supper?   _____
Do homework?   _____
Watch TV?   _____
Go to bed?   _____

Time yourself like this for 3 or 4 days.

For the rest of the days, write what you did in the mornings, afternoons, and evenings.

_____ Bear credit
_____/_____ Date and signature for
_____ Arrow point credit

d. Write an invitation to someone.

Do you know a boy who could be a Cub Scout? Invite him to your den meeting.

Has your teacher ever come to a pack meeting? Send your teacher an invitation to your next pack meeting. Make your teacher an honorary member of your den.

Do you know what R.S.V.P. on an invitation means? It stands for words in the French language which mean "Please reply."

_____ Bear credit

____/_____ Date and signature for
_____ Arrow point credit

e. Write a story about something you have done with your family.

You can tell your story just the way it happened; or, you can pretend you have your own time machine. Set the controls to any time in history from caveman to astronaut. One story might be meeting Robin Hood and Little John in Sherwood Forest.

Do four achievements for YOURSELF

____/_____
____ Bear credit
Date and signature for
____ Arrow point credit

f. Write a thank-you note.

When someone gives you a present, that's the time to write a thank-you note.

There are other times when you are invited to:
- Dinner
- The movies
- Go swimming

A thank-you note is always appreciated.

_____ Bear credit
_____ / _____ Date and signature for
_____ Arrow point credit

g. Write about the doings of your den.

Your pack may have its own newspaper and its editor would like to have your story for the paper. If there isn't a pack paper, tack your story on the bulletin board.

_____ Bear credit
_____ / _____ Date and signature for
_____ Arrow point credit

CUB SCOUT LEADER BALOO SAYS: When you have done five of the requirements, have a parent or an adult sign here.

_____ / _____ Date and signature for achievement 18.

19

Shavings and chips

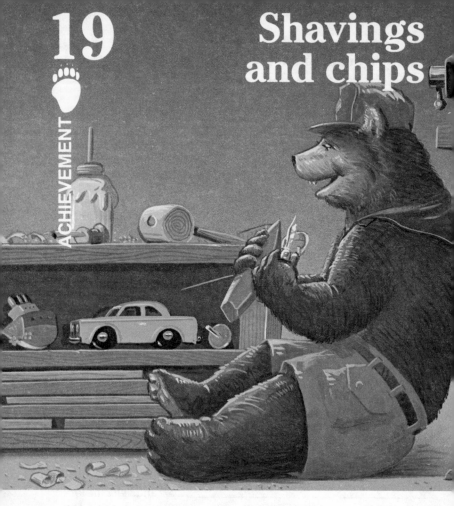

Your Cub Scout knife is an important tool. You can do many things with its four blades. The cutting blade is the one you will use most of the time. With it you can make shavings and chips to carve all kinds of things.

You must be very careful and think when you whittle or carve. Take good care of your knife. Always remember that a knife is a tool, not a toy. Use it with care so that you don't hurt yourself or spoil what you are carving.

REQUIREMENTS

Do all of the following requirements:

a. Know the safety rules for handling a knife.

SAFETY RULES

- A knive is a tool, not a toy.
- Know how to sharpen a knife. A sharp knife is safer because it is less likely to slip and cut you.
- Keep the blade clean.
- Never carry an open knife in your hand.
- When you are not using your knife, close it and put it away.
- Keep your knife dry.
- When you are using the cutting blade, do not try to make big shavings or chips. Easy does it.

____ Bear credit

____/_____ Date and signature for

____ Arrow point credit

b. Show that you know how to take care of and use a pocketknife.

SHARPENING A KNIFE. Lay the blade on a sharpening stone as though you were going to shave a thin sliver from the stone. Push the blade forward. Turn the blade over and shave the stone toward you. Pushing down hard is not necessary. Continue this back and forth action until the edge looks like a line without bright spots. Bright spots on the blade are knicks that reflect the light. You can see a dull edge; you can't see a sharp one.

b. Continued

SHARPENING STICK. If you don't have a sharpening stone, you can use a sharpening stick. Look at the picture to see how to make one. Cover a stick with a piece of inner tube. Tack it down. Cover the inner tube with emery cloth and tack it down as shown.

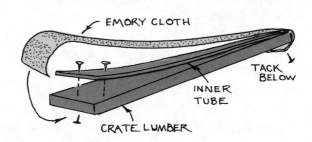

Do four achievements for YOURSELF

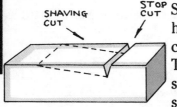

SHAVINGS AND CHIPS. You don't have to be strong to whittle and carve, but you have to be smart. Take it easy. Make a lot of small shavings and cuts. Here is the secret: before you make a shaving cut, make a stop cut. At the place you want the shaving to stop, cut straight down with your knife. Press down and rock the blade back and forth until the cut is as deep as you want it to go. Then make the shaving cut into it and lift away the shaving.

_____ Bear credit
_____/_____ Date and signature for
_____ Arrow point credit

c. Make a carving with a pocketknife. Work with your parent or den leader in doing this.

TRACE PATTERN

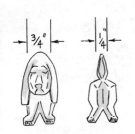

Eskimos carve beautiful animals from walrus ivory. They make seals, bears, dogs, and people. You can make a carving of a bear that looks like an Eskimo carving. Carve it out of soap.

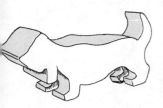

MAKE BOTH SIDES THE SAME

3/4"   1/4"

FRONT AND BACK VIEWS

_____ Bear credit

_____ / _____ Date and signature for

_____ Arrow point credit

d. Earn the Whittling Chip card.

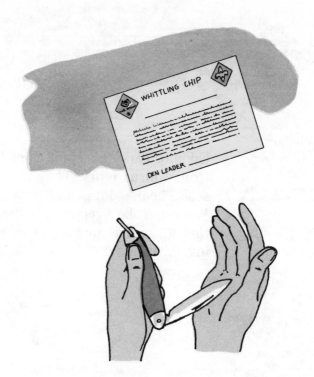

KNIVES ARE NOT TOYS

- Close the blade with the palm of your hand.
- A knife should never be used on something that will dull or break it.
- Be careful that you do not cut yourself or any person nearby.
- A knife should never be used to strip the bark from a tree.
- Do not carve your initials into anything that does not belong to you.

POCKETKNIFE PLEDGE

- I understand the reason for safety rules.
- I will treat my pocketknife with the respect due a useful tool.
- I will always close my pocketknife and put it away when not in use.
- I will not use my pocketknife when it might injure someone near me.
- I promise never to throw my pocketknife for any reason.
- I will use my pocketknife in a safe manner at all times.

____/_____

____ Bear credit

Date and signature for

____ Arrow point credit

CUB SCOUT LEADER BALOO SAYS: When you have done all the requirements, have a parent or an adult sign here.

____/_____ Date and signature for achievement 19.

20

Sawdust and nails

CLUB HOUSE

DEN MEETING

TUE 4:00

W hen you can cut wood to the right length and fasten it together with nails, you are a handy-man; but there are more tools than a hammer and saw. You will need something to hold the wood in place while you work on it. Sometimes you will need to make a curved cut or put a hole through the wood.

A good way to learn how to use tools is to watch someone using them. When you need to make something with wood ask your parent or an adult to show you how to use the tools safely.

WARNING: Do not use electrical tools, unless an adult helps you.

REQUIREMENTS

Do all of the following requirements:

a. **Show how to use and take care of four of these tools.**

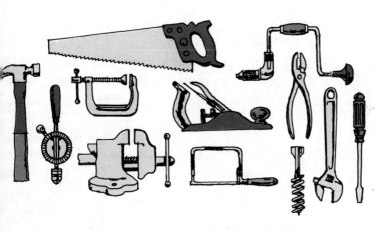

_____ CRESCENT WRENCH. This open-end wrench can be adjusted to fit many sizes of nuts.

_____ COPING SAW. Lets you cut curves.

_____ "C" CLAMP. Holds pieces of wood together for gluing.

_____ HAND SAW. There are two kinds: one for cross cutting, and another for ripping lengthwise along the grain of the wood.

_____ BIT. Corkscrew-shaped drills are called bits. They are used to drill holes in wood.

_____ BRACE. Holds the bits for drilling holes in wood.

a. Continued

____ HAND DRILL. Works like an egg beater and uses twist drills to bore holes in wood and metal.

____ HAMMER. Used for driving nails, for prying boards apart, and for pulling nails.

____ BENCH VISE. Holds wood in place for sawing or planing.

____ WOOD PLANE. Smoothes rough boards.

____ SCREW DRIVER. Sets screws.

____ PLIERS. Slip joint pliers have wide and normal jaw openings to grip different size things. (Don't use pliers on nuts—use a crescent wrench instead.)

____ Bear credit

____/_____ Date and signature for

____ Arrow point credit

b. Build your own tool box.

You will need three pieces of wood 1 by 6 inches. Two side pieces are 20 inches long. The bottom is 18 inches long.

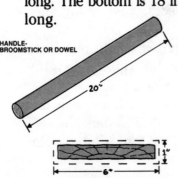

HANDLE-
BROOMSTICK OR DOWEL

20"

6"

The ends are made of the same 1- by 6-inch wood and are 8 inches long. Corners are cut off and a hole drilled large enough for the broomstick handle. Parts can also be cut from ¾-inch plywood.

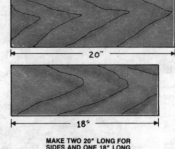

1" x 6" BOARDS

20"

18"

MAKE TWO 20" LONG FOR
SIDES AND ONE 18" LONG
FOR BOTTOM

Did you know—wood sizes are measured when boards are still rough? When the rough edges are cut off, the board really measures smaller. Your 1-inch board is really ¾ inch thick.

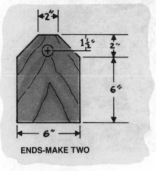

2"

1½" 2"

6"

6"

ENDS-MAKE TWO

____ Bear credit
____/_____ Date and signature for
____ Arrow point credit

c. Use at least two tools listed in requirement *a* to fix something.

____ Bear credit
____/_____ Date and signature for
____ Arrow point credit

CUB SCOUT LEADER BALOO SAYS: When you have completed all three requirements, have a parent or an adult sign here.

____/_____ Date and signature for achievement 20.

21

Build a model

Model kits can be fun to put together. You can be proud of your model when it is finished. Most boys like to put together models. Did you know that you might still be putting models together when you grow up?

Many grownups like to build models as a hobby. They build ships out of wood, or large model train layouts they call "pikes."

Models are also used by companies for serious purposes. Auto makers build small models of their new cars before they actually start making them. Companies that build airplanes do the same thing. People who design and build shopping centers or other kinds of buildings often build models to see what the building will look like. Model buildings can be serious business for grownups. You can see, model building can be more than just going to the hobby shop and buying a kit.

REQUIREMENTS

Do three of the following requirements:

1. Build a model from a kit.

This can be any kind of model. Follow the directions and customize it any way you like.

_____ Bear credit

___/_____ Date and signature for

_____ Arrow point credit

2. Build a display for one of your models.

If your model is a boat, mold soft clay around the boat up to the water line. Remove the boat. After the clay has hardened, paint it blue to make it look like water with waves and whitecaps.

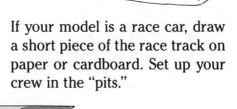

If your model is a race car, draw a short piece of the race track on paper or cardboard. Set up your crew in the "pits."

b. Continued

If your model is a dinosaur, make a jungle using clay, leaves, and twigs.

_____ Bear credit
_____/_____ Date and signature for
_____ Arrow point credit

c. Make believe you are planning to change the furniture layout in one of the rooms in your home.

Draw the outline of a room on a piece of paper. On another piece of paper draw the outlines of the furniture. Draw your room and furniture cutouts to the scale of ½ inch = 1 foot. Use the paper cutouts on your room drawing to plan the changes. See how much easier it is to move your cutouts around than it is to move the furniture.

Models let us see what the real thing will look like before it is made.

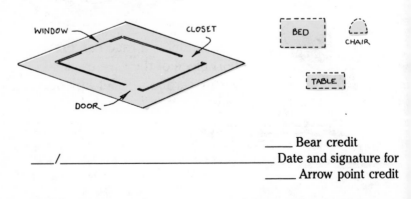

_____ Bear credit
_____/_____ Date and signature for
_____ Arrow point credit

d. Make a model of a mountain, a meadow, a canyon, or river.

Use dirt, sand, stones, sticks, twigs, and grass cuttings.

_____ Bear credit
_____/_____ Date and signature for
_____ Arrow point credit

.

e. Look at a model of a shopping center or new building that is on display somewhere.

That model may have been built to help plan the construction. It may have also been used to show the project to community leaders.

_____ Bear credit
_____/_____ Date and signature for
_____ Arrow point credit

f. Make a model of anything—a rocket, boat, car, or plane.

Use whatever you want to make it.

_____ Bear credit
_____/_____ Date and signature for
_____ Arrow point credit

CUB SCOUT LEADER BALOO SAYS: When you have done three of the requirements, have a parent or an adult sign here.

_____/_____ Date and signature for achievement 21.

Tying it all up

S ailors, cowboys, and mountain climbers all use good strong rope. Their lives may depend on their ropes and the knots that hold them in place.

REQUIREMENTS

Do five of the following requirements:

a. Whip the ends of a rope.

Ropes are made of twisted fibers. As long as the rope is in one piece, the fibers stay in place; but when the rope is cut, the fibers in the two ends begin to straighten out. Whip them in place with string or wrap with tape.

WHIP A ROPE. Start with a piece of twine or cotton fishing line 2 feet long. Make it into a loop and place it at one end of the rope. Wrap the twine tightly around the rope starting ¼ inch from the rope end. When the whipping is as wide as the rope is thick, pull out the ends hard and trim off the twine or fishline.

____ Bear credit
____/_____ Date and signature for
____ Arrow point credit

b. Tie a square knot, bowline, sheet bend, two half hitches, and a slip knot. Tell how each knot is used.

SQUARE KNOT. A common knot made with two overhand knots. Square knots are used in first aid to tie bandages.

BOWLINE. A knot to make a nonslipping loop at the end of the rope. It is a rescue knot when tied around your waist.

SHEET BEND. This knot looks like a bowline; but instead of making a loop, it joins ropes of different sizes.

TWO HALF HITCHES. This knot is used to tie a rope to a post, tree, or a ring.

SLIP KNOT. This knot slips easily along the rope around which it is made. The knot itself is a simple overhand knot. It can be used to tie a rope to a post. Can also be used to tie a package.

_____ Bear credit

_____/_____ Date and signature for

_____ Arrow point credit

c. Learn how to keep a rope from tangling.

Before you put a rope away, lay the rope out straight on a dry surface. Be sure there are no kinks or knots in it. Hold the end of the rope in one hand and coil the rope around your forearm from hand to elbow. Loop it around as many times as necessary to take up all of the rope. Take it off your elbow, hold the coil in your hand and take off one loop with your other hand. Make a few turns around the coils with this end and pass it through the top of the coil held by your hand.

_____ Bear credit

_____/_____ Date and signature for

_____ Arrow point credit

d. Coil a rope. Throw it, hitting a 2-foot square marker 20 feet away.

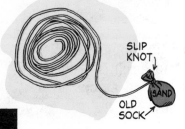

SLIP KNOT
SAND
OLD SOCK

Put a weight on the end of your rope, heavy enough to carry your line out when you throw it.

Coil your rope in 1-foot loops. Hold half the loops and the weighted line in your throwing hand. Hold the other loops in your other hand.

Face the marker and swing the line toward it. Keep trying until you can hit the mark. It is important that you become good at this because someday you may need to rescue a person from drowning.

_____ Bear credit

____/_____ Date and signature for
_____ Arrow point credit

Do four achievements for YOURSELF

e. Learn a magic rope trick.

When you fold your hands across your chest and pick up a rope end with each hand, you have tied an overhand knot just by holding the ends and unfolding your hands.

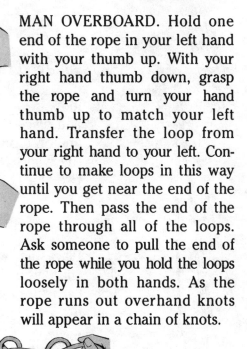

MAN OVERBOARD. Hold one end of the rope in your left hand with your thumb up. With your right hand thumb down, grasp the rope and turn your hand thumb up to match your left hand. Transfer the loop from your right hand to your left. Continue to make loops in this way until you get near the end of the rope. Then pass the end of the rope through all of the loops. Ask someone to pull the end of the rope while you hold the loops loosely in both hands. As the rope runs out overhand knots will appear in a chain of knots.

____ Bear credit
____/_____ Date and signature for
____ Arrow point credit

f. Make your own rope.

Use 24 feet of binder twine. Put the ends alongside each other and tie them in an overhand knot.

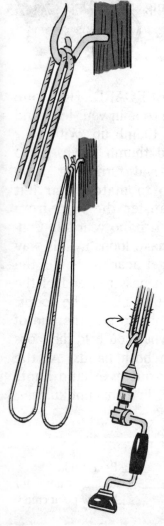

Clamp a large nail in a bench vise and loop the knotted end of the twine over the nail. Soak the line thoroughly before you start.

Pull the twine loop out straight until you get to the end of the loop. Now go back to the nail and place the loop over the nail and on top of the knotted end of the twine. Now pull back on the two loops to their ends.

Place the two blocks on a hook that you have placed in a carpenter's drill brace. Using the brace and pulling back slightly to keep the twine tight, twist the four strands of twine together tightly until they choke up around the nail and hook. Keep the twisting line straight by pulling back on the brace.

Place a chair or stool where you are standing and rest the brace on its seat. Use the weight of the brace to keep your new rope straight.

Now for the hard part: Let the rope dry for 24 hours! Remove from the nail and hook and whip each end.

With an adult, singe the loose fibers from the rope.

___/_____

____ Bear credit

Date and signature for

____ Arrow point credit

CUB SCOUT LEADER BALOO SAYS: When you have done five of the requirements, have a parent or an adult sign here.

___/_____ Date and signature for achievement 22.

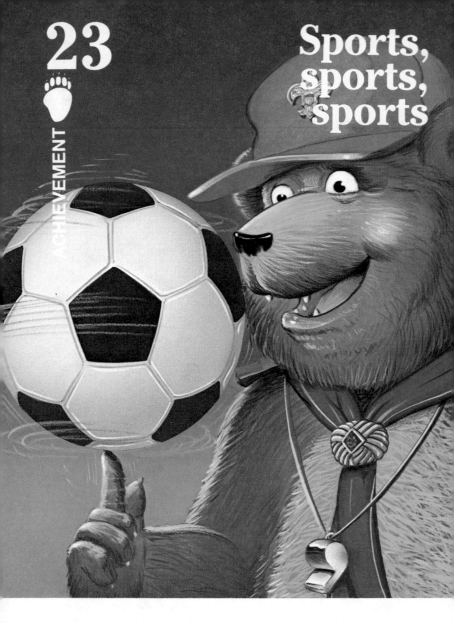

Sports make for great times. They help us stay healthy and in good shape. They are fun to watch and fun to play.

REQUIREMENTS

Do all of the following requirements:

a. Learn the rules and how to play three team sports.

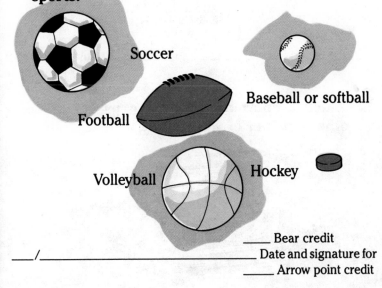

Soccer

Baseball or softball

Football

Volleyball

Hockey

____/_____
____ Bear credit
Date and signature for
____ Arrow point credit

b. Learn the rules and how to play two sports in which only one person is on each side.

Tennis, racquetball, darts, ping-pong, badminton, and golf are examples of individual sports.

____/_____
____ Bear credit
Date and signature for
____ Arrow point credit

c. Take part in one team and one individual sport.

____ _____
Team Sport

____ _____
Individual Sport

____ Bear credit
____/_____ Date and signature for
____ Arrow point credit

d. Watch a sport on TV with a parent or some other member of your family.

Do four achievements for YOURSELF

Discuss the rules and how the game was played.

____ Bear credit
____/_____ Date and signature for
____ Arrow point credit

e. Attend a high school, college, or professional sporting event with your family or your den.

Did the players show good sportsmanship?

Did the spectators?

_____ Bear credit

____/_____ Date and signature for
_____ Arrow point credit

CUB SCOUT LEADER BALOO SAYS: When you have done all of the requirements, have a parent or an adult sign here.

____/_____ Date and signature for achievement 23.

eadership means more than just telling others what to do. It means doing the right things. It also means listening to everyone's ideas before going ahead.

It's hard to be a leader, but you feel good if you do your job well.

Your community and country need good leaders. In these requirements you will find some ways to be a good leader.

REQUIREMENTS

Do three of the following requirements:

a. Help a boy join the Cub Scouts, or help a new Cub Scout through the Bobcat trail.

Do you know any boys your age who are not Cub Scouts?
Being interested in others is the mark of a leader.

____ Bear credit
____/_____ Date and signature for
____ Arrow point credit

b. Serve as a denner or assistant denner.

Denner_____ from_____ to_____

Assistant
Denner_____ from_____ to_____

____ Bear credit
____/_____ Date and signature for
____ Arrow point credit

c. Plan and conduct a den activity with the approval of your den leader.

Den activity_____

_____

____ Bear credit
____/_____ Date and signature for
____ Arrow point credit

____/_____ Den leader's signature

d. Tell two people they have done a good job.

For example:
- A Cub Scout leads a good ceremony

- A classmate does well on an assignment

- A parent helps your den with an outing

____ Bear credit
____/_____ Date and signature for
____ Arrow point credit

e. Leadership means choosing a way even when your choice is not liked by all.

Talk about these hard choices with one of your parents or an adult. What would you do if it were up to you?

- It is time to go home, but you are having a good time with your friends and they don't have to be home until 30 minutes later. What do you do?

_____

- Your friends are going to ride their bikes to the other side of town, and they ask you to go with them. You know you are not allowed to do that. What do you say to them?

_____

- A new boy has moved into the neighborhood. How do you become his friend?

_____

- While your class is taking a test, the teacher leaves the room. Some of the students start trading test answers. Do you?

_____

- What if another student asks you for an answer?

_____

- Is it hard to keep from cheating?

_____

CUB SCOUT LEADER BALOO SAYS: When you have done three of the requirements, have a parent or an adult sign here.

____/_____ Date and signature for achievement 24.

NOW FOLLOW MY

Arrow Point Trail

Now you are a Bear Cub Scout. Wait! You can still have lots of fun with your *Bear Book*. Baloo has electives for you to do. Electives are not like achievements. You can pick any requirement you like from the electives and do it. When you have completed 10 electives, you have earned your first arrow point, a gold one. After earning a Gold Arrow Point, you may complete 10 more requirements to earn a Silver Arrow Point. Under your Bear badge, you may wear as many Silver Arrow Points as you earn.

When working on the achievements to earn your Bear badge, you may have seen some requirements you wanted to try but didn't. Now you can review the Achievements section of your *Bear Book* and use any requirement you did not count toward your Bear badge. These achievement requirements now follow the same rules as the elective requirements. Each one is a separate project. You can mix requirements from electives and unused achievements in any manner to get the ten you need for each arrow point.

You may earn arrow points from the *Bear Book* until you become 10 years old, or until you complete the fourth grade, when you will join a Webelos den.

Remember this important rule: If you completed an achievement requirement to earn your Bear badge, you cannot use it again to earn arrow points. But there are lots more.

Space

What do you see when you look toward the sky? You might say, "In the daytime, I see the sun and the clouds. At night, I see the moon and stars."

That's true, of course. You also are looking at man's newest frontier.

Here's your chance to learn something about space.

REQUIREMENTS

__a. **Identify two constellations and the North Star.**

__b. **Make a pinhole planetarium and show three constellations.**

__c. **Visit a planetarium.**

__d. **Build a model of a rocket or space satellite.**

__e. **Read and talk about at least one man-made satellite and one natural one.**

__f. **Find a picture of another planet in our solar system. Explain how it is different from Earth.**

NO.	DATE	ADULT SIGNATURE	✓ DEN CHART
1.			
1.			
1.			
1.			
1.			
1.			

AROW POINT TRAIL

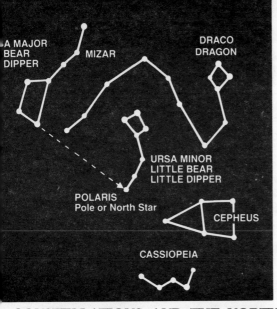

CONSTELLATIONS AND THE NORTH STAR. Groups of stars have names. One star group looks like a W. Another looks like a saucepan or a Big Dipper. The two stars in the bowl of the Big Dipper point to the North Star. Constellations punched as holes in tin cans may be used as pinhole planetariums.

SATELLITES. Satellites are small objects that move around bigger ones. The moon is a satellite of the Earth. Some of our TV and radio programs are bounced off man-made satellites placed in orbit by the space shuttle.

Weather ELECTIVE **2**

Everybody wants to know what the weather is and what it will be tomorrow. Will it rain out my team's baseball game? Do I need a sweater? Those are questions you probably have asked.

In this elective, you will learn how weather forecasts are made, how to measure rain and snowfall, and how to figure wind directions.

REQUIREMENTS

__a. **Learn how to read a thermometer. Put a thermometer outdoors and read it at the same time every day for 2 weeks. Keep a record of each day's temperature and a description of the weather each day (fair, rain, fog, snow, etc.).**

__b. **Build a weather vane, record wind direction for 2 weeks at the same hour. Keep a record of the weather for each day.**

__c. **Make a rain gauge. Record rainfall for 2 weeks.**

__d. **Find out what a barometer is and how it works. Tell your den about it. Tell what "relative humidity" means, too.**

__e. **Learn to identify three different kinds of clouds. Estimate their height.**

__f. Watch the weather forecast on television every day for 2 weeks. Describe three different symbols used on weather maps. Keep a record of how many times the weather forecast is correct.

NO.	DATE	ADULT SIGNATURE	✓ DEN CHART
2.			
2.			
2.			
2.			
2.			
2.			

For your outdoor thermometer, build a box with pieces of an old slatted shutter for sides. This will keep the sun away from it but let air in.

Set it up facing north. It should be about 4 feet off the ground so the thermometer is easy for you to see. Make your temperature reading at the same time every day. Mark it on your chart.

DATE	TEMP.	WEATHER	WIND

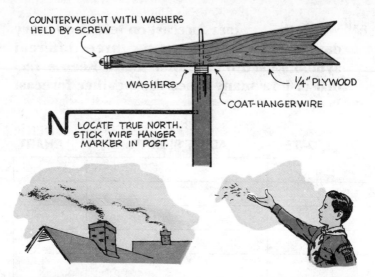

COUNTERWEIGHT WITH WASHERS HELD BY SCREW

WASHERS

1/4" PLYWOOD

COAT-HANGER WIRE

LOCATE TRUE NORTH. STICK WIRE HANGER MARKER IN POST.

WEATHER VANE. Weather forecasters describe the wind by the direction it is coming FROM—not the direction it is going. The pointed end of your vane points toward the direction the wind is coming from. If you forget, look at the smoke from chimneys and you can see it blowing away from the wind. Toss up a few blades of grass and see which way they go. Check the wind direction at the same regular times as you check your temperature and rain gauges. Mark it on your chart.

CAN MUST BE LEVEL.

BE SURE CAN WON'T BLOW OFF.

CAN ABOUT 30 INCHES ABOVE GROUND.

TO MAKE MEASURING JAR, POUR 1" OF WATER IN CAN. POUR IN OLIVE JAR AND MARK 1" DIVIDE INTO 10THS.

RAIN GAUGE. Use a large juice can (1 quart, 14 ounces). Set it on a platform with sides to keep it from blowing away. Choose an open place in your yard. Take your reading at the same time every day, morning or evening. If there isn't enough to measure in the can, pour the water from the can into your measuring jar.

Snowfall is measured by how much water it makes. Melt the snow caught and measure it in your jar. One inch of water equals about 10 inches of snow.

You can measure snow on the ground by sticking your ruler or yardstick into several spots. Write each measurement down. Add them up and divide by the number of measurements. (Ask for help with this one.) This gives you the average depth of snow.

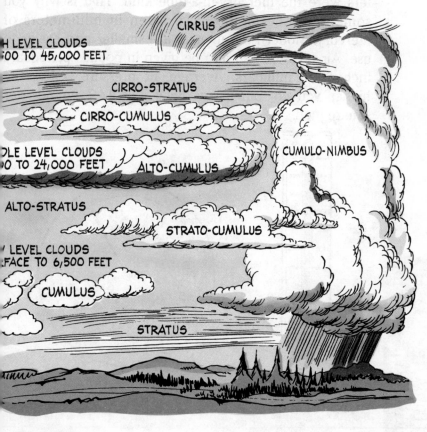

CIRRUS

H LEVEL CLOUDS
OO TO 45,000 FEET

CIRRO-STRATUS

CIRRO-CUMULUS

CUMULO-NIMBUS

DLE LEVEL CLOUDS
O TO 24,000 FEET   ALTO-CUMULUS

ALTO-STRATUS

STRATO-CUMULUS

LEVEL CLOUDS
FACE TO 6,500 FEET

CUMULUS

STRATUS

BAROMETER. Weather forecasters use a barometer to help predict whether it's going to rain or whether a nice day is coming.

Forecasters can do this because the barometer measures air pressure. Air pressure, or weight of the air, helps them learn whether it will be fair or rainy. Warm air is lighter than cold air and is more likely to bring a storm.

Changes in air pressure can be seen on either mercury in a tube or on a metal bellows. These small motions can be magnified to give the air pressure. Early barometers were the mercury-in-a-tube kind. That is why you sometimes see air pressure given in millimeters of mercury. Modern barometers are smaller and easier to use. Air pressure can also be given in pounds per square inch or in millibars. Average air pressure is less the higher you go, but at sea level it is 14.7 pounds per square inch.

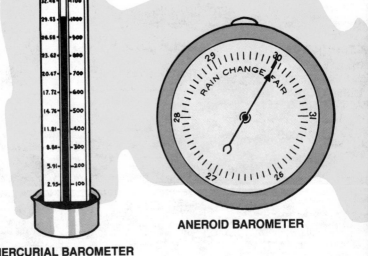

MERCURIAL BAROMETER

ANEROID BAROMETER

RELATIVE HUMIDITY. Relative humidity is the term weather forecasters use to tell how much moisture is in the air. If there is a lot of moisture in the air, the relative humidity will be a high figure, like 70 or 80. If the air is dry, it will be much lower like 20 or 30.

On a summer day, if the temperature is 85 degrees and the relative humidity is 80, you will feel hot and sticky. On a day when it's cooler, that much humidity won't bother you at all. It will be a pleasant day.

The weather forecaster finds the figure for relative humidity by comparing the amount of moisture in the air with the amount it could hold if saturated at the same temperature.

Radio

You probably hear a radio every day without thinking much about it. Radio is just one of the things you have grown up with.

When radio first began, however, everyone thought it was wonderful that music and words could be sent all over the world without wires.

You can find out for yourself the excitement of the early days of radio, and learn how it works by building a radio set for yourself.

REQUIREMENTS

__a. **Build a crystal or diode radio. Check with your local craft or hobby shop or in the *Boys' Life* ads. It is all right to use a kit.**

__b. **Make and operate a battery powered radio following directions with the kit.**

NO.	DATE	ADULT SIGNATURE	✓ DEN CHART
3.			
3.			

ARROW POINT TRAIL

Many good kits are on sale for making crystal sets. This is the first kind of radio that was invented. They get their power from the radio signal, so you will need a long, high antenna to make yours work. Even with a good antenna, there will be only enough power for a small earphone.

A transistor or tube radio can also be built from a kit. This kind of radio gets its power from a battery, so it may be able to operate a loudspeaker. Ask an adult to help you. Follow directions carefully, and you'll have a thrill of "tuning in on the world."

Hang a map on the wall (one you have pasted on cardboard) and keep track of all the stations you get.

Maybe you know someone who is an amateur radio operator or "ham." Ask to see his transmitter and receiver. Ask about some of the far-away places he has talked with by radio.

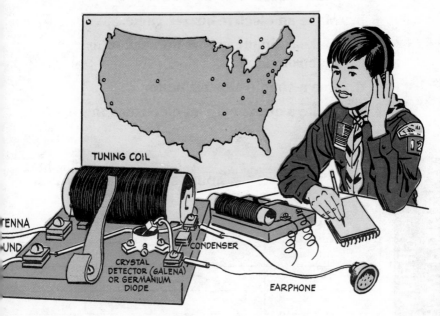

TUNING COIL

ANTENNA

GROUND

CRYSTAL DETECTOR (GALENA) OR GERMANIUM DIODE

CONDENSER

EARPHONE

Electricity

Wouldn't it be fun to make an electric motor that really works? Well, you can.

There are other things like games and toys that run on electricity which you can also make.

As you build them, you will be learning about electricity, the power that runs so many things around your house and school and around your community.

REQUIREMENTS

__a. **Wire a buzzer or doorbell.**

__b. **Make an electric buzzer game.**

__c. **Make a simple bar or horseshoe electromagnet.**

__d. **Use a simple electric motor.**

__e. **Make a crane with an electromagnetic lift.**

NO.	DATE	ADULT SIGNATURE	✔ DEN CHART
4.			
4.			
4.			
4.			
4.			

Did your doorbell ever get out of order? Sometimes when it happens, it's just because the connections are loose or the wires are corroded. If you know how to wire a doorbell, you will probably know how to fix it. You can mount a doorbell buzzer on a piece of wood to learn how to wire it. Get someone to work with you on this.

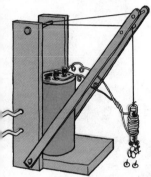

Electromagnets take some skill to make but are a lot of fun. You can make all kinds of tools and electric games with them. Get your dad or some other adult to work with you on this.

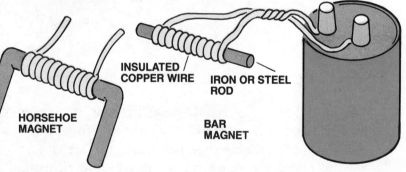

HORSEHOE MAGNET

INSULATED COPPER WIRE

IRON OR STEEL ROD

BAR MAGNET

Make up a separate sounding board. Use on many games. Make a question-and-answer board for your teacher. You can use it for many quizzes. Write the questions and answers on sticky tape, change them as often as you wish.

Any number of electric games can be made using a

buzzer, a bell, or a flashlight bulb. We've shown you a few basic types. Now invent your own.

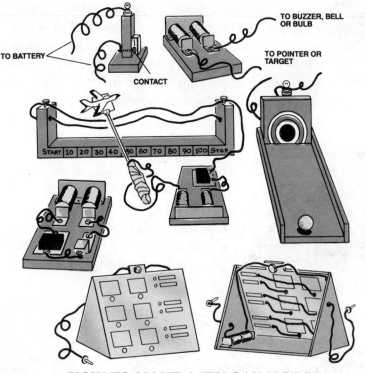

HOW TO MAKE A TIN CAN MOTOR

From the rotor pattern on page 167, cut five pieces of tin. Drill center hole to fit snugly on 2¼-inch finishing nail. Fasten five pieces together with adhesive tape.

Wind magnet wire on rotor until space is nearly full. Leave 2 inches at ends of winding.

Wind ½ inch adhesive tape on nail close to rotor. Make about ¼ inch in diameter.

Cut two tin strips ½ by ¼ inch to mold around adhesive tape, each covering about one-fourth of surface. Scrape wire ends of winding and wrap each end around one of the tin strips. Fasten in place by ⅛ inch strip of adhesive tape.

Cut tin 3¾ by 9 inches, fold five times to ¾ inch width, and hammer flat. Bend to this shape.

Wind several layers of the wire around the top of field, leaving a few inches on each side for connections.

Brushes made from strand wire wrapped around tin strip. Connect field wire to base. Fold tin strips to ½ inch width to form uprights. Put hole in only one side to support nail. For power, connect to three dry cell batteries or toy transformer.

ROTOR

MMUTATOR

D, BRUSHES AND ASSEMBLY

Boats

Boating and sailing are great sports. Maybe you have already been sailing, but do you know how to rig a sailboat? Make a raft? Repair a dock? Do you know the safety rules for boaters?

If your answers were no, find out now. Anchors aweigh!

REQUIREMENTS

__a. **Help your dad or any other adult rig and sail a real boat.**

__b. **Help your dad or any other adult repair a real boat or canoe.**

__c. **Know storm warning flag signals.**

__d. **Help your dad or any other adult repair a boat dock.**

__e. **Know the rules of boat safety.**

__f. **With an adult, demonstrate forward strokes, turns, and backstrokes. Row a boat around a 100-yard course involving two turns.**

NO.	DATE	ADULT SIGNATURE	✓ DEN CHART
5.			
5.			
5.			
5.			
5.			
5.			

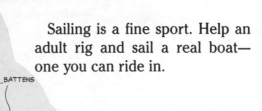

Sailing is a fine sport. Help an adult rig and sail a real boat—one you can ride in.

Labels on the sailboat diagram:
BATTENS, RUNNING BACKSTAY, JIBSTAY, JIB, MAIN HALYARD, MAINSAIL, MAST, BOOM, TILLER, JIB SHEET, KEEL, CENTERBOARD, MOTOR BRACKET, RUDDER, TRANSOM

You get credit in this elective by helping your parent or any other adult fix up a boat dock. Check for loose boards, nails that are sticking up, or splinters that may cause an accident and injure someone.

ELECTIVE 5

Repairing a boat or canoe is a good thing to be able to do. You'll be a proud Cub Scout, if you are able to help a boat owner make repairs.

1. To repair your canvas canoe, sandpaper the break. Smooth the edges all around.

2. Apply marine glue or varnish.

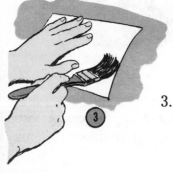

3. Cover with fine cloth (muslin) patch and varnish.

STORM WARNINGS. The weather bureau uses a combination of flags and pennants to warn boaters of approaching storms.

Small-Craft Warning. One red flag by day and a red light above a white light at night.

SMALL CRAFT

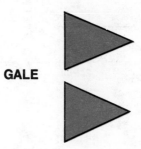

Gale Warning. Two red pennants by day and a white light above a red light at night.

GALE

Whole-Gale Warning. A single square red flag with a black center by day and two red lights at night.

WHOLE GALE

Hurricane Warning. Two square red flags with black centers by day and a white light between two red lights at night.

HURRICANE

ELECTIVE 5

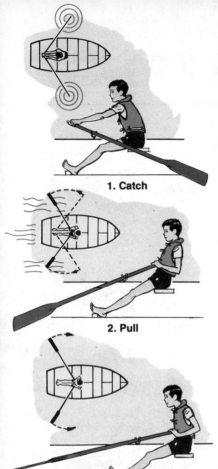

1. Catch

2. Pull

3. Feather

4. Recover

BOATING. Grasp the oar handles firmly, knuckles up, wrists and arms straight, body bent forward.

Catch. Lower oar blades edgewise into water, not too deep.

Pull. Lean backward, pulling on the oars and bending your arms until your elbows come in against your ribs.

Feather. Lift oar blades slightly out of water and turn your knuckles up toward your face so that the blades are flat to the water's surface.

Recover. Bend forward and straighten wrists and arms, ready to begin another stroke.
To do the backstroke, push on the oars instead of pulling.
To turn, pull on one oar while you hold the other in the water

as a pivot or push it in the opposite direction.

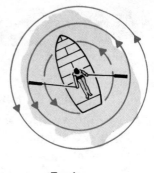

Turning

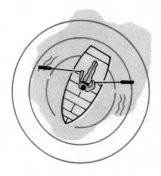

BOAT SAFETY

1. Know your boat—don't overload it. In a rowboat, one person per seat is a pretty safe rule.
2. Balance your load. Distribute weight evenly from side to side and from bow to stern.
3. Step into your boat. Step in the center when boarding or changing seats, keeping low. Take a life preserver for each passenger in the boat. Be sure to wear them.
4. If your boat capsizes or swamps, hang on. You can kick the boat to shore or drift in, but don't leave it, let help come to you.
5. Watch the weather. Head for shore when it looks stormy. If you are caught out, seat your passengers on the floor and head your boat into the waves.
6. If you use a motor, use the right one. Too much power can damage your boat or swamp it. Look on your boat's transom for the OBC (Outboard Boating Club of America) plate showing boat capacity and recommended maximum horsepower. Avoid sharp turns—they are hard on equipment and people. Take it easy.

Aircraft

Cub Scouts are too young to fly real airplanes, but they can learn a lot about them.

They can fly model airplanes. They can visit airports, talk to pilots, and be a passenger in an airplane.

There are lots of ways to have fun with airplanes, and to learn more about them.

REQUIREMENTS

__a. **Identify five different kinds of aircraft in flight, if possible, or from models or photos.**

__b. **Ride in an airplane (commercial or private).**

__c. **Explain how a hot air balloon works.**

__d. **Build and fly a model airplane. (You can use a kit. Every time you do this differently, it counts as a completed project.)**

__e. **Sketch and label an airplane showing the direction of forces acting on it (lift, drag, and load).**

__f. **What are some of the things a helicopter can do that other kinds of airplanes can't? Make a list. Draw or cut out a picture of a helicopter and label the parts.**

__g. **Build and display a scale airplane model. You may use a kit or build it from plans.**

NO.	DATE	ADULT SIGNATURE	✔ DEN CHART
6.			
6.			
6.			
6.			
6.			
6.			
6.			

HOT AIR BALLOONS. The first successful flying machines were hot air balloons. We fly them today for sport, but they still work the same way. Air has weight, just like everything else made of matter.

Air, and other gases, expand when they are heated. A plastic bag of hot air will weigh less than a plastic bag of cool air. The plastic bag of hot air will try to rise, like a bubble in water, because the cooler, heavier air around it tries to push in and occupy the same space. This is how a hot air balloon works. Some balloons use other kinds of gas, like helium, which is already lighter than air without being heated.

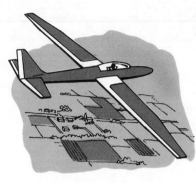

THERMALS. When the sun heats the ground, a layer of air near the surface is heated too, and rises in a current of warm air called a thermal. In the same way, warm air from a fire rises up the chimney, drawing in fresh air for the fire and carrying the smoke away. Sailplane pilots find these invisible rising currents and ride them.

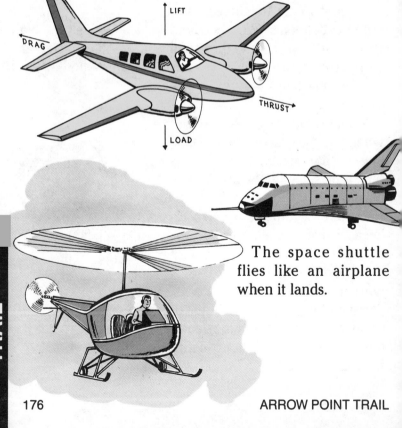

The space shuttle flies like an airplane when it lands.

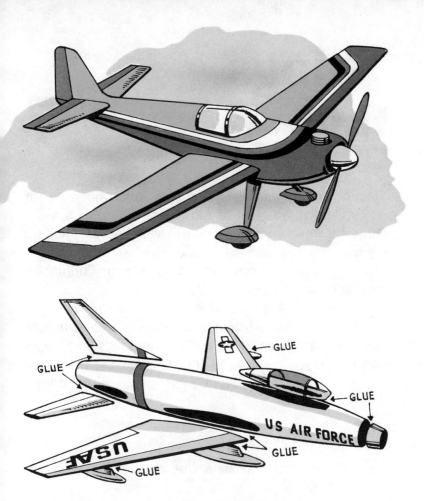

Lots of stores sell kits for making scale model planes that fly and solid models that don't. The kits have instructions telling you how to put the parts together. After a little practice with these, you can design and build your own special model.

Things that go

ELECTIVE 7

Maybe when you were little, your folks got you a toy car to ride. It was lots of fun. Think how much fun it would be now if you built your own! You can build it any way you like, and stop, go, or steer as you please.

On the next page you'll see plans for your Cubmobile. Try it and have fun.

Cubmobiles are not the only things that go. Have you ever seen a windmill or a water wheel and wondered what they do? Here are plans for windmills and water-wheels that you can make. After you've done them, you may want to make an invention of your own that goes.

REQUIREMENTS

__a. **Make a scooter or a Cubmobile. Know safety rules.**

__b. **Make a windmill.**

__c. **Make a waterwheel.**

__d. **Make an invention of your own design that goes.**

ARROW POINT
TRAIL

                    ARROW POINT TRAIL

NO.	DATE	ADULT SIGNATURE	DEN CHART
7.			
7.			
7.			
7.			

CUBMOBILE

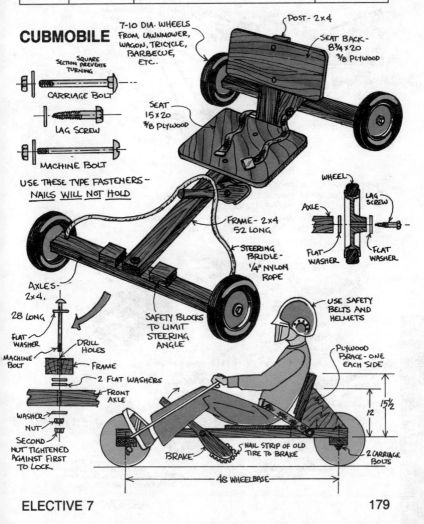

7-10 DIA. WHEELS FROM LAWNMOWER, WAGON, TRICYCLE, BARBECUE, ETC.

POST- 2×4

SEAT BACK- 8¾×20 ⅜ PLYWOOD

SECTION PREVENTS TURNING — SQUARE

CARRIAGE BOLT

LAG SCREW

MACHINE BOLT

USE THESE TYPE FASTENERS - <u>NAILS</u> <u>WILL</u> <u>NOT</u> <u>HOLD</u>

SEAT 15×20 ⅜ PLYWOOD

WHEEL

AXLE

LAG SCREW

FLAT WASHER

FLAT WASHER

FRAME- 2×4 52 LONG

STEERING BRIDLE- ¼" NYLON ROPE

AXLES- 2×4, 28 LONG

FLAT WASHER

MACHINE BOLT

DRILL HOLES

FRAME

2 FLAT WASHERS

FRONT AXLE

WASHER

NUT

SECOND NUT TIGHTENED AGAINST FIRST TO LOCK

SAFETY BLOCKS TO LIMIT STEERING ANGLE

USE SAFETY BELTS AND HELMETS

PLYWOOD BRACE- ONE EACH SIDE

15½

12

BRAKE

NAIL STRIP OF OLD TIRE TO BRAKE

2 CARRIAGE BOLTS

48 WHEELBASE

ELECTIVE 7

179

SIDEWALK SAFETY RULES

- Pedestrians have the right of way.

- Watch out for cars coming out of driveways.

- Don't carry passengers.

- Don't ride in the street.

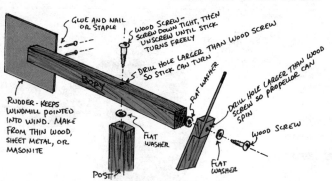

GLUE AND NAIL OR STAPLE

WOOD SCREW — SCREW DOWN TIGHT, THEN UNSCREW UNTIL STICK TURNS FREELY

DRILL HOLE LARGER THAN WOOD SCREW SO STICK CAN TURN

BODY

FLAT WASHER

DRILL HOLE LARGER THAN WOOD SCREW SO PROPELLOR CAN SPIN

WOOD SCREW

RUDDER - KEEPS WINDMILL POINTED INTO WIND. MAKE FROM THIN WOOD, SHEET METAL, OR MASONITE

FLAT WASHER

POST

FLAT WASHER

PEOPLE HAVE USED WINDMILLS FOR THOUSANDS OF YEARS TO GRIND GRAIN AND PUMP WATER. TODAY WE ARE LEARNING TO USE THE WIND TO MAKE ELECTRIC POWER. WINDMILL BLADES MUST BE AT AN ANGLE TO THE DIRECTION OF THE WIND TO WORK. THE FASTER THE WIND BLOWS, THE FASTER YOUR WINDMILL WILL TURN.

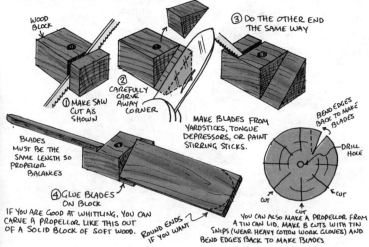

WOOD BLOCK

① MAKE SAW CUT AS SHOWN

② CAREFULLY CARVE AWAY CORNER

③ DO THE OTHER END THE SAME WAY

MAKE BLADES FROM YARDSTICKS, TONGUE DEPRESSORS, OR PAINT STIRRING STICKS.

BLADES MUST BE THE SAME LENGTH SO PROPELLOR BALANCES

④ GLUE BLADES ON BLOCK

IF YOU ARE GOOD AT WHITTLING, YOU CAN CARVE A PROPELLOR LIKE THIS OUT OF A SOLID BLOCK OF SOFT WOOD.

ROUND ENDS IF YOU WANT

BEND EDGES BACK TO MAKE BLADES

DRILL HOLE

CUT

CUT

CUT

YOU CAN ALSO MAKE A PROPELLOR FROM A TIN CAN LID. MAKE 8 CUTS WITH TIN SNIPS (WEAR HEAVY COTTON WORK GLOVES) AND BEND EDGES BACK TO MAKE BLADES

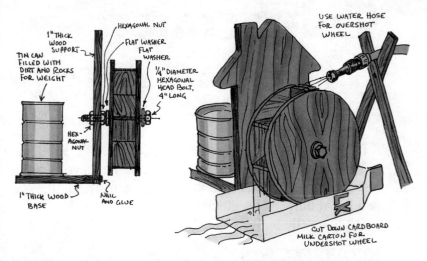

USE WATER HOSE FOR OVERSHOT WHEEL

1" THICK WOOD SUPPORT

HEXAGONAL NUT

FLAT WASHER
FLAT WASHER

TIN CAN FILLED WITH DIRT AND ROCKS FOR WEIGHT

¼" DIAMETER HEXAGONAL HEAD BOLT, 4" LONG

HEXAGONAL NUT

1" THICK WOOD BASE

NAIL AND GLUE

CUT DOWN CARDBOARD MILK CARTON FOR UNDERSHOT WHEEL

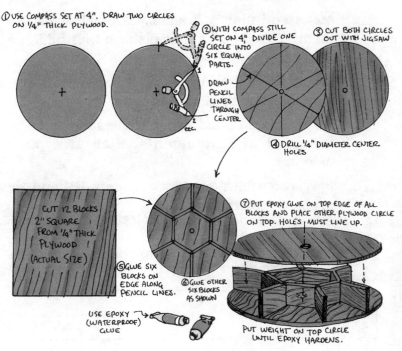

① USE COMPASS SET AT 4". DRAW TWO CIRCLES ON ¼" THICK PLYWOOD.

② WITH COMPASS STILL SET ON 4" DIVIDE ONE CIRCLE INTO SIX EQUAL PARTS.

DRAW PENCIL LINES THROUGH CENTER

③ CUT BOTH CIRCLES OUT WITH JIGSAW

④ DRILL ¼" DIAMETER CENTER HOLES

CUT 12 BLOCKS 2" SQUARE FROM ¼" THICK PLYWOOD (ACTUAL SIZE)

⑤ GLUE SIX BLOCKS ON EDGE ALONG PENCIL LINES.

⑥ GLUE OTHER SIX BLOCKS AS SHOWN

USE EPOXY (WATERPROOF) GLUE

⑦ PUT EPOXY GLUE ON TOP EDGE OF ALL BLOCKS AND PLACE OTHER PLYWOOD CIRCLE ON TOP. HOLES MUST LINE UP.

PUT WEIGHT ON TOP CIRCLE UNTIL EPOXY HARDENS.

Cub Scout band

Here comes the band—the Cub Scout band!

You can play music even if you have never had a lesson. You can even make your own instrument. You can learn how in this elective.

Strike up the band!

REQUIREMENTS

__a. **Make and play a homemade musical instrument—cigarbox banjo, washtub bull fiddle, a drum or rhythm set, tambourine, etc.**

__b. **Learn to play two familiar tunes on an ocarina, a harmonica, or a tonette.**

__c. **Play in a den band using homemade or regular musical instruments. Play at a pack meeting.**

__d. **Play two tunes on any recognized band or orchestra instrument.**

NO.	DATE	ADULT SIGNATURE	✔ DEN CHART
8.			
8.			
8.			
8.			

Wanting to learn to play music is all you need to get started. Try the simple instruments first until you find one you'd like to play well. Then, PRACTICE.

If you are lucky enough to be studying with a music teacher, keep it up. Remember, you must practice to play well.

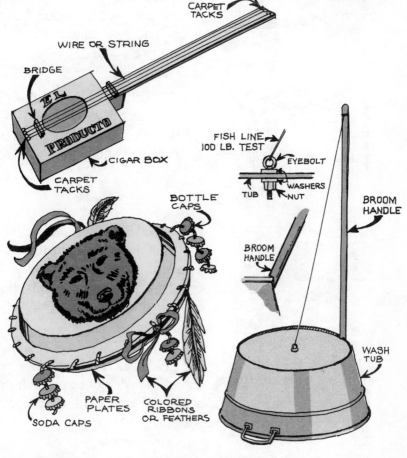

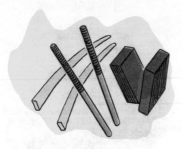

STICKS, BONES, and BLOCKS.
Use ½-inch and 1-inch dowels 8
and 12 inches long. Notch some
of them. Clean and dry short ribs
of beef. Make hand size sandpaper blocks.

RATTLES. Use gourds, spice
boxes, small cans, shells, coco-
nuts, paper tubes, or paper sacks
for rattles. Put in dried beans,
peas, noodles, macaroni, sand,
buttons, or beads.

TRIANGLES. Use brass pipe, 12
inches long. Strike with solid brass
rod, 6 inches long. Horseshoe and
spike. Pencil and glass.

DRUMS. Use canvas, inner tube,
or animal skin for drumheads.
The drum body could be a tin
can, ice-cream carton, cereal box,
or fiber drainpipe.

BOTTLE FLUTE. Put empty on
a tray in order of size. Each one
sounds different. Tune by adding
water.

Bottles all tuned, rubber bands all in place, strings all tightened up, washboard handy—OK, strike up the band! Homemade bands are lots of fun. With a little practice you can get sweet music out of the simplest things.

Go to your library for more ideas or ask your music teacher at school. They can probably suggest some things to make, too.

Art

Art is not just pictures. The artist's skill is used to make pictures and sculpture that tell a story and are pleasant to look at. That is what art is all about. Statues and stained glass windows are made for the same reasons. Study the art around you, and try your hand at making your own.

REQUIREMENTS

__a. **Do an orginal art project and show it at a pack meeting. Every project you do counts as one requirement. Some ideas for art projects are:**

Mobile or Wire sculpture	**Acrylic painting**
Collage	**Clay sculpture**
Silhouette	**Water color**
Mosaic	**Silk screen picture**

__b. **Visit an art museum or picture gallery with your den or family.**

NO.	DATE	ADULT SIGNATURE	✔ DEN CHART
9.			
9.			
9.			
9.			
9.			
9.			

MOBILE. To make a mobile you will need:

Three pieces of coathanger wire, different lengths

Four cardboard shapes (any shape you like)

Heavy thread or light fishing line

Fisherman's swivel

Pair of pliers

Icepick or nail for punching holes in cardboard

Step 1. Form a small loop in both ends of each piece of wire, using pliers.

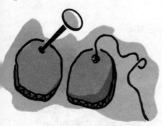

Step 2. Make a hole near the edge of each cardboard shape, using the nail or icepick. Tie a short piece of line to each cardboard piece.

Step 3. Tie a piece of cardboard to the loops in both ends of the shortest piece of wire. Tie an 8-inch piece of line at the center.

Step 4. Slide wire back and forth until it balances on the center line. Bend it at the balance point. This makes a small angle so the line will not slide back and forth.

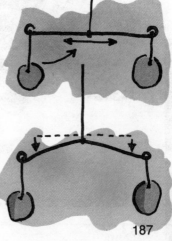

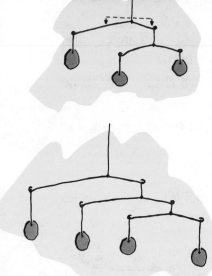

Step 5. Tie this assembly to one end of the medium-length wire. Tie cardboard pieces to the ends. Tie an 8-inch line in the middle. Balance and bend the same way you did in step 4.

Step 6. Repeat step 5, using the longest wire and the assembly you made in step 5. Tie the hanging line to the fisherman's swivel. Use it to hang your mobile where it will be free to turn in air currents. The slightest breeze will make it turn and form ever-changing patterns.

A COLLAGE is a picture made up of bits of other pictures. The pieces are pasted up to make a new piece of art.

188

To make a SILHOUETTE, tape a piece of white paper to the wall. A person sitting in front of a bright light casts a shadow on the paper. Trace around the shadow with a pencil. Take the paper off the wall, lay it on a sheet of black construction paper, and cut through both sheets along the pencil line you have traced. Paste the black silhouette cutout on a piece of white paper for display.

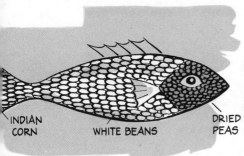

INDIAN CORN   WHITE BEANS   DRIED PEAS

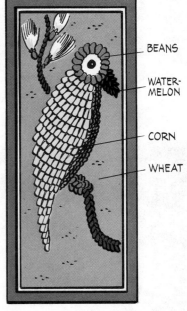

BEANS

WATER-MELON

CORN

WHEAT

A MOSAIC is a picture made of tiny bits of stone, tile, or glass cemented into a pattern. You don't need to use stone and tile; you can glue bits of broken glass, marbles, or seeds to a piece of plywood to make your mosaic. Use white glue.

Masks

Since time began we have been using masks to act out plays, games, and important religious ceremonies. We wear masks to pretend we are something besides ourselves. This can be fun, like Halloween.

REQUIREMENTS

__a. **Make a simple papier-mâché mask.**

__b. **Make an animal mask.**

__c. **Make an American Indian mask.**

__d. **Make a clown mask.**

NO.	DATE	ADULT SIGNATURE	✓ DEN CHART
10.			
10.			
10.			
10.			

PAPIER-MÂCHÉ MASKS. These may be made on an oval dish. Turn it upside down and grease it so the mask won't stick when you're through. Tear newspapers into strips. Make a paste with flour and water. Make it quite thick—about as heavy as pea soup. Now you are ready. Dip the paper strips into the paste mixture.

First start to build the head with layers of paper strips pasted together. To build up eyebrows, noses, lips, and cheeks, hold wads of newspaper in place and paste them down with long strips of paper.

BALL

WIRE →

After the mask is dry, paint the features. You can use a rubber ball for the clown's nose and rope, yarn, or brown straw for hair.

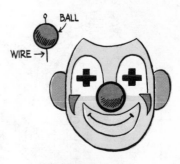

PAPER BAG MASKS. Use a large grocery bag. Cut eye holes and draw face with a felt tip pen. Cut another bag into strips. Curl the strips and glue them to the lion's head to make the lion's mane.

Glue two bags together to make a bull's head.

STYROFOAM
OR
CARDBOARD

GLUE TWO
SACKS
TOGETHER
TO MAKE
NOSE

MILK JUG MASKS. Cut bottle in two with knife or scissors. Trim off screw cap. Each half can be used top or bottom side up to give four different face shapes.

Handle side (handle up) can be used for a knight's helmet, or for

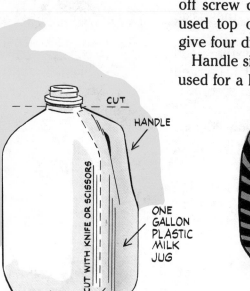

PHAROAH

TIGER

"The Man in the Iron Mask," sprayed with metallic paint. Remove a portion or all of the handle, add cardboard ears, and you have a dog, bear, or other animal. Turn over and paint gold. It looks like an Egyptian pharoah, with a high forehead and ornamental head covering. Paint orange, add black stripes, pointed ears, cardboard nose, and presto, a tiger. Painted black, with broom straw whiskers, a "purr-fectly" terrific cat appears.

The other half can be used to make an owl, bird, or space creature. Make a knight or a clown, or paint green to make a Martian. Many muppet characters can be made from this half.

Cut out eye holes and mouth shapes with a knife or model-building knife. Glue on construction paper decorations. Use your imagination; glue on bits of styrofoam, yarn, fake fur, toothpaste caps, toothpicks, soda straws, or whatever you can find.

FOZZIE BEAR

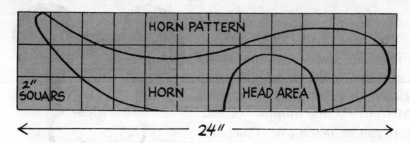

HORN PATTERN

2" SQUARS

HORN   HEAD AREA

← ———————— 24″ ———————— →

PUEBLO MASK. This is a Hopi Indian mask, a Hopi *kachina*, or spirit. Copy the horn pattern on cardboard. Draw 2-inch squares on the cardboard to help you draw. Make two pieces just alike. Make fringe by wrapping black yarn around a piece of cardboard (figure 1). Make six or seven loops. Tie together and take off cardboard (figure 2). When you have enough loops, staple them around the horn (figure 3). Glue the other horn shape over this, making a "sandwich" with the yarn between the two pieces (figure 4). Weight it down. When dry, staple along the edges to hold fringe. Clip the loops (figure 5). Paint the horn. Use tempera or acrylic paint.

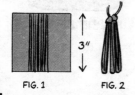

3″

FIG. 1   FIG. 2

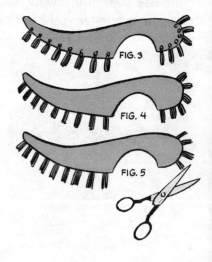

FIG. 3

FIG. 4

FIG. 5

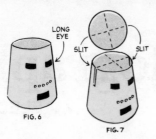

FIG. 6

FIG. 7

The headpiece is made from a cardboard paint bucket, large enough to go over your head and sit on your shoulders. Poke a row of breathing holes 3 inches up from the lip (figure 6).

Mark the sides and cut horn slits on both sides. Slits are ½-inch wide and 4½ inches long, as near the top as possible (figure 7). Gently push the horn through, opening up the slit if you need to. Try on the mask and mark your eye level. Take mask off and cut two eye slits, 1½- by ¾-inch.

The mask and the horn are white. Make the "eyes" and "mouth" from ¾-inch-wide black plastic electrical tape. Notice that the left eye goes out to the end of the horn. Make a fuzzy "wig" from black yarn fringe, like you made for the horn, but use a 6-inch card and don't cut the loops. Tape to top. Add feathers. Stuff an old nylon stocking with rags to make collar. Cut 1-inch strips of cloth and wind them around collar. Tape to mask.

BLUEJAY FEATHERS

LONG EYE

FEATHER

EYE HOLES

Photography
ELECTIVE 11

Taking pictures is a lot of fun, but it can be harder than you may think. You need to use a camera to learn the secrets of making good pictures.

REQUIREMENTS

__a. **Practice holding a camera still in one position. Learn to push the shutter button without moving the camera. Do this without film in the camera until you have learned how. Look through the viewfinder and see what your picture will look like. Make sure that everything you want in your picture is in the frame of your viewfinder.**

__b. **Take five pictures of the same subject in different kinds of light.**
  (1) Subject in direct sun with direct light.
  (2) Subject in direct sun with side light.
  (3) Subject in direct sun with back light.
  (4) On a sunny day, subject in shade.
  (5) Cloudy day.

__c. **Put your pictures to use.**
  (1) Mount a picture on cardboard for display.
  (2) Mount on cardboard and give it to a friend.
  (3) Make three pictures that show how something happened (tell a story) and write one sentence explanation for each.

___d. Make a picture in your house.
  (1) With available light.
  (2) Using a flash attachment or photo flood.

NO.	DATE	ADULT SIGNATURE	✔ DEN CHART
11. ·			
11.			
11.			
11.			

IMPROVE YOUR PHOTOS BY CROPPING. Crop (or trim) your pictures so they show only the main subjects. Crop out background that does not matter.

The more pictures you take the more you'll notice that the ones you like best tell a story. The subject is doing something besides posing. The action tells something about the subject.

BEFORE
CROPPING

AFTER
CROPPING

PICTURE HINTS

There should be bright light, if possible.

The camera must be steady.

Wind the film right after you snap the picture.

Every good picture has a center of interest.

If possible, take the picture of your subject against a good background.

Store negatives in transparent envelopes, not regular paper ones.

BACK LIGHT   SIDE LIGHT   DIRECT SUN

TOO FAR AWAY

DON'T TILT THE CAMERA

GOOD

BUSY BACKGROUND

CONTRAST GOOD

AGAINST A POST

ON A ROCK OR CHAIR

DIRECTION OF ACTION

BLUR

GOOD

NO ACTION

Nature crafts

ELECTIVE **12**

When you go on a hike with a group in the woods, watch for animal tracks. Look at the trees and see how many you can name. If you look carefully, you will see that the rocks are many shapes, sizes, and colors.

Nature is a fun world to get to know.

REQUIREMENTS

__a. **Make shadow prints or blueprints of three kinds of leaves.**

__b. **Make a display of eight different animal tracks with an eraser print.**

__c. **Collect, press, and label 10 kinds of leaves.**

__d. **Collect, mount, and label 10 kinds of insects.**

__e. **Collect eight kinds of plant seeds and label.**

__f. **Collect, mount, and label 10 kinds of rocks or minerals.**

__g. **Collect, mount, and label five kinds of shells.**

__h. **Make a spider web print; mount and display it.**

NO.	DATE	ADULT SIGNATURE	✔ DEN CHART
12.			
12.			
12.			
12.			
12.			
12.			
12.			
12.			

You can buy ozalid paper at a blueprint or surveyor supply store. Place a leaf on the ozalid paper, cover with glass, and expose to sunlight. Roll the ozalid paper into a cardboard tube and place over a jar lid filled with ammonia to develop your leaf print.

OZALID PAPER AT BLUEPRINT STORE OR SURVEYOR'S SUPPLY STORE

GLASS

① LEAF

OZALID PAPER (COATED SIDE UP)

② EXPOSE TO SUNLIGHT

③ ROLL INSIDE CARDBOARD TUBE, DEVELOP BY SITTING ON JAR LID FILLED WITH HOUSEHOLD AMMONIA.

Use a stamp pad and a pencil eraser to print animal tracks. Study the animal tracks you find in the sand and mud along streams and mud puddles.

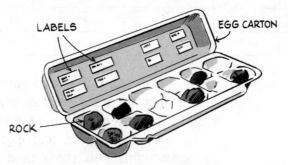

SHELL AND ROCK COLLECTIONS. Keep your collection in empty egg cartons. This will protect the shells from breakage. It will keep rocks from scratching shelves or furniture. At the start, you can just use the bottom half of a carton. Later, use both the top and bottom. Label each item.

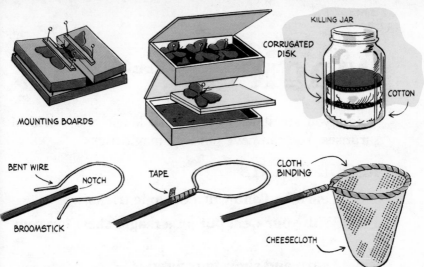

MOUNTING BOARDS

KILLING JAR

CORRUGATED DISK

COTTON

BENT WIRE

NOTCH

TAPE

CLOTH BINDING

BROOMSTICK

CHEESECLOTH

INSECTS. Shown above are things you will need to collect and mount insects. When you catch an insect in the net, hold it with the cloth and push the killing jar up into the net. Drop the bug into the jar and quickly put the top on. The insect will die quickly. Then mount it in your specimen box.

SPIDER WEB PRINT. Spray spider web with two or three coats of hair spray. Transfer the web to a sheet of black construction paper while the last coat is still wet.

HAIR SPRAY

Magic

Now you see it—now you don't! Magic is a world of surprises. You can have fun with magic tricks.

REQUIREMENTS

__a.   **Learn and show three magic tricks.**

__b.   **With your den, put on a magic show for your pack.**

__c.   **Learn and show four puzzles.**

__d.   **Learn and show three rope tricks.**

NO.	DATE	ADULT SIGNATURE	✓ DEN CHART
13.			
13.			
13.			
13.			

Look in your *Boys' Life* magazines and the *Cub Scout Magic* book for more magic tricks.

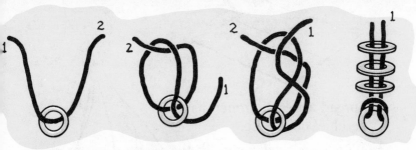

STRING THE WASHERS. One washer is knotted to the center of the string. Next the two ends of the string are raised, and the rest of the washers dropped on so they fall on the knotted washer.

The two ends of the string are separated, and each end is given to a helper.

Place a hankerchief over the washers. Reach under the hankerchief and pull all the washers out.

The trick is in the tying of the knot.

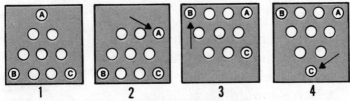

| 1 | 2 | 3 | 4 |

TRIANGLE TURNABOUT PUZZLE. Put 10 checkers or 10 coins on a table. Arrange them in a triangle pointing toward you. Don't put them close together (figure 1).

Tell the audience the checkers or coins are flying saucers leaving their home base. Say they want to turn around and fly back home. Only three of them can fly in straight lines to make a new triangle pointing away from you.

Let your friends have plenty of time to try to do it. Remember, they can move only three items, and all must move in straight lines.

Show them how by making the moves shown in figures 2, 3, and 4.

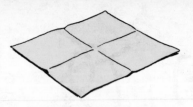

1. Spread a freshly ironed handkerchief on a table.

2. With your right hand, lift the center so it stands by itself.

3. Lift to show nothing is under it.

4. Spread over the left hand.

5. Lift at center, it stands on your hand.

6. Again with your right hand, lift to show nothing is supporting it.

7. In your left hand you have a metal tape measure. It is hidden by the back of your hand, which is toward the audience.

8. Drape the handkerchief over your left hand. Turn your hand, palm upward; grasp the end of the ruler through the handkerchief and pull out. The handkerchief will be standing in the air.

9. Push the center of the handkerchief down with the right hand. Pocket the handkerchief and metal tape with left hand.

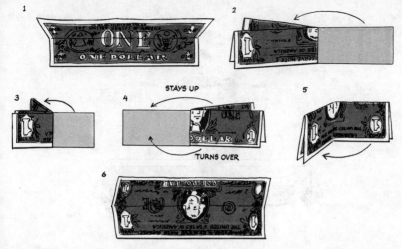

MAGIC DOLLAR. Say this as you fold and unfold a dollar bill: "If you had nothing to do, day in and day out, but look out of a dollar bill; you would probably think up something to do. George Washington likes to stand on his head, see . . ."

Then with the bill facing the audience, fold it in half lengthwise.

1. Fold the top half forward.

2. Fold the right half forward to the left.

3. Fold the right half forward—to the left again.

4. Unfold the back half of the bill (the two corners) to the right.

5. Swing the front half of the bill to the left. Bring the front portion of the bill upward, and you're right back where you started.

6. Fold exactly as you did before, but in step 5 swing the back half of the bill to the left, lift the front part of the bill, and old George is standing on his head.

How about that! (A new, stiff bill will make this trick easier.)

THE FLOATING BODY. Were you ever in a big crowd at a parade where you thought you saw a young boy who was taller than a grown-up? And then, when you got closer, you saw that it was really a very small boy seated on his father's shoulders.

Well, that was an illusion. You thought you saw something strange, but it really wasn't.

Magicians use illusions all the time. One of the best is the floating body trick. And with practice you can do it, too.

Here's what you need: a helper; a large bed sheet; a towel; two sticks, 3 or 4 feet long; and a pair of shoes and socks just like the helper is wearing.

Fasten the shoes and socks on the sticks. Tie the sticks together. Roll a towel lengthwise and tie it on sticks to give them shape. They are supposed to be the helper's legs and should have some shape.

You will need a long low bench that your helper can straddle. Place a cover over this so it reaches the floor on the audience's side. The fake legs are on the floor on the side toward you.

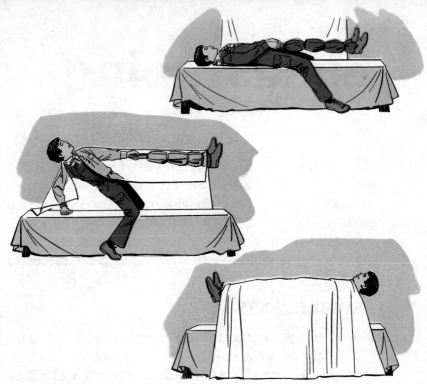

To perform the trick:

1. Have helper seat himself on the bench with one leg on each side.

2. Hold the sheet between the bench and the audience.

3. Helper puts false legs in place and lies on the bench.

4. Cover him with the sheet so that only his head and the fake feet stick out.

5. The helper places his right hand on the bench and slowly stands up with his head back, as if he were still lying down. He holds the sticks level with his left hand and raises them as he stands. This is startling if done slowly. It looks as if he is floating in air.

The trick looks hard but, with practice, the helper will be able to rise easily.

Landscaping

ELECTIVE **14**

Some of our most useful plants are food plants. Other plants are grown for their beauty. Deciding which plants to use and how they should be arranged is called landscaping.

Careful use of flowers, bushes, and trees can make our homes, neighborhoods and parks nicer places to live and visit.

REQUIREMENTS

__a. **Help your parents take care of your lawn or help take care of the lawn of a public building, school, or church. Seed bare spots. Get rid of weeds. Pick up litter. Agree ahead of time on what you will do.**

__b. **Make a sketch of a landscape plan for the area right around your house or for an apartment building. Talk it over with your parents or den leader. Show what trees, shrubs, and flowers you could plant to make the area look better.**

__c. **Take part in a project with your family, den, or pack to make your neighborhood or community more beautiful. These might be cleanup parties, painting, planting, cleaning and painting trash barrels, and removing ragweed. (Each time you do this differently, it counts as a completed project.)**

__d. **Build a greenhouse and grow 20 plants from seed. You can use a package of garden seeds, or use beans, pumpkin seeds, or watermelon seeds.**

NO.	DATE	ADULT SIGNATURE	DEN CHART ✓
14.			
14.			
14.			
14.			

YOUR FLOWER GARDEN. Make your flowerbed interesting. Don't plant in rows but in groups as in this picture. Don't put all flowers of one kind or color in one spot. Light flowers in front of dark ones are the most pleasing. Plant small flowers like violets and pansies in front of taller ones like hollyhocks and zinnias.

ZINNIAS

HOLLYHOCKS

PANSIES

VIOLETS

Plant your garden rows running as nearly north and south as possible so the plants will get lots of sun. If the ground is sloping, the rows should run crosswise as shown. This is called *contour* planting. If the rows run up and down hill, rain will wash away the soil. This is called *erosion*.

BEAUTIFY YOUR NEIGHBORHOOD. Help plan for a small arrangement of bushes, shrubs, or flowers around the flagpole in your schoolyard.

Maybe the planting of a few shrubs along the block would help make the street where you live a more pleasant place.

Why not plant the kinds of things that attract birds? Here are a few:

Bushes—Barberry, bayberry, high bush, blueberry, elderberry, mulberry, common privet, staghorn sumac, viburnam, black haw, doublefile, and yew.

Trees—Box elder, birch, red cedar, flowering crab, dogwood, fir, hemlock, white pine, maple, mountain ash, wild cherry, and spruce.

ARROW POINT TRAIL

CLEAR
PLASTIC
BAG

SIMPLE
GREENHOUSE

POTTING
SOIL OR
RICH DIRT

Plant seeds in dirt. Add about 1 cup of water. Tie up and leave in a sunny spot until the seeds sprout.

POTTING SOIL
OR RICH DIRT

Start seeds in an egg carton. Put in miniature greenhouse.

MINIATURE GREENHOUSE. Make a greenhouse from ¾-inch wood strips. Use white glue and small box nails. Cover with heavy, clear plastic. Tack or staple. Fits over a cookie sheet.

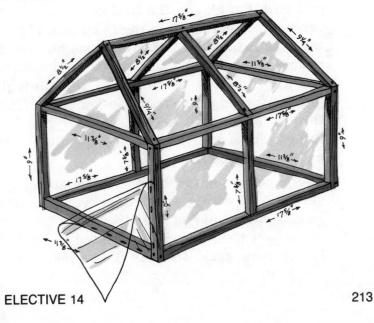

ELECTIVE 14

Water and soil conservation

ELECTIVE 15

Every living thing depends on clean water and rich earth. It is important that we learn as soon as we can how to care for our water and soil.

REQUIREMENTS

__a. Dig a hole or find an excavation project and describe the different layers of soil you see and feel. (Do not enter an excavation area without permission.)

__b. Take three cans the same size and punch four holes in the bottom of each with a hammer and nail. Put clay in the first can, soil in the second can, and sand in the third can. Fill all three cans one-half full. Pour one-half can of water into each can, one at a time. Write down the time it takes the water to run through (until dripping stops) each kind of earth. (The three kinds of earth are not good for growing things alone, but when mixed together they make very good soil.)

__c. Visit a burned-out forest or prairie area, or a slide area, with your den or your family. Talk to a member of the U.S. Forest Service about how the area will be planted and cared for, to grow again the way it was before the accident.

__d. Some people like to use live Christmas trees. After Christmas, plant the tree in your yard, or at school, your Boy Scout council service center, or a park. Find out all the things you need to know about how to take care of a live Christmas tree in your home.

__e. What is wind erosion? Find out the kinds of grass, trees, or ground cover you need to plant to stop wind erosion.

__f. As a den, visit a lake, stream, river, or ocean (whichever is nearest to where you live). Plan a den project to help clean up this important source of water. Name four kinds of water pollution.

NO.	DATE	ADULT SIGNATURE	✓ DEN CHART
15.			
15.			
15.			
15.			
15.			
15.			

Soil is very important to you. Almost all your food and clothing come from plants that grow in the soil and from animals that eat them.

SAND   SOIL   CLAY

FILL CANS TO SAME LEVEL

PUNCH HOLES IN BOTTOM WITH NAIL

Farm animals

You can learn more about farm animals even if you don't live on a farm or a ranch. If you do, it is easier, but if not, you can find pictures of different farm animals in magazines and learn how they are used. You can read a book about farm animals. Then when you go for a ride in the country, you will know what kinds of cattle, horses, pigs, and sheep you see.

REQUIREMENTS

__a. **Take care of a farm animal. Decide with your parent the things you will do and how long you will do them.**

__b. **Name and describe six breeds of farm animals and tell their common uses.**

__c. **Read a book about a farm animal and tell your den about it.**

__d. **With your family or den, visit a livestock exhibit at a county or state fair.**

NO.	DATE	ADULT SIGNATURE	✓ DEN CHART
16.			
16.			
16.			
16.			

JERSEY

HOLESTEIN

GUERNSEY

ABERDEEN-ANGUS

SHORTHORN

HEREFORD

HAMPSHIRE

POLAND CHINA

MERINO

RHODE ISLAND RED

LEGHORN

DUCK

RIDING HORSE

PLYMOUTH ROCK

Repairs ELECTIVE 17

It seems as though there is always something that needs fixing around the house. Who takes care of these repairs where you live? Maybe you have already helped with repair work. If not, ask before you try. Talk it over. Make sure you understand what to do before you start. Electrical and plumbing jobs are not games. You have to know what you are doing.

REQUIREMENTS

__a. **With the help of an adult, fix an electric plug or an electrical appliance.**

__b. **Use glue or epoxy to repair something.**

__c. **Remove and clean a drain trap.**

__d. **Refinish or repaint something.**

__e. **Agree with your parent on some repair job to be done and do it. (Each time you do this differently, it counts as a completed project.)**

NO.	DATE	ADULT SIGNATURE	✔ DEN CHART
17.			
17.			
17.			
17.			
17.			

HOW TO FIX A PLUG OR SOCKET. With some help, you can make repairs on light switches, sockets, and plugs. Be sure the cord is disconnected before you start work on the other end.

Learn to tie the underwriter's knot. It takes the strain off the connection. To tie it make a loop with the white wire. Run the black wire through the loop around the white wire, then back up through the loop. Scrape off the insulation on the ends of both wires and connect them to the screws. Tighten the screws. Pull the wire up snug and replace the insulator shield if there is one.

Take a light socket apart by pressing the metal shell below the cap.

Thread wire through the cap and tie underwriter's knot. Scrape wire and wrap ends around screws. Tighten the screws. Pull the wire snug in the cap. Replace the metal shell and snap in place.

Be sure your hands and the floor are dry before you plug in the lamp or turn on the switch.

HOW TO CLEAN A DRAIN TRAP. A drain trap is a U-shaped piece of pipe in a sink drain that gives a low spot to hold water. This keeps gas from the sewer from coming into the house. Sometimes it clogs up and it must be taken off and cleaned out.

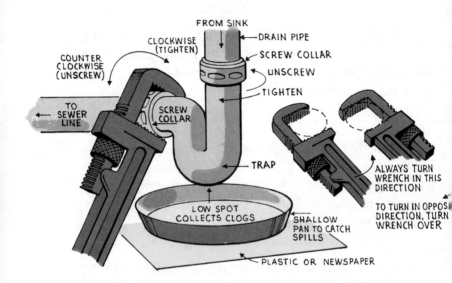

To clean a trap, first put down plastic sheeting or newspaper below the trap. The trap is full of water, so protect the area beneath the sink from spills. Use a pan to catch any drips.

Use a large pipe wrench to loosen the two screw collars that hold the trap. They have right-hand threads, which means that you turn them clockwise (the way a clock's hands move) to tighten them. You will need to turn them the other way (counterclockwise) to unscrew them. They may be tight to start with, so you will need help from an adult with this job. After each collar has been unscrewed two or three times with the pipe wrench, you can probably unscrew them the rest of the way by hand.

When both collars are completely unscrewed, you can lift out the trap. Be careful; it is full of water, soap scum, and other trapped things that you won't want to spill. First, unscrew one collar and hold the trap with one hand while you unscrew the second collar by hand, so it won't fall off when the collar loosens.

Carefully place the trap in the pan so it won't spill. Carry it to where you can dump it. The water can be poured into another drain, but the sludge and solid material should go in the trash. Flush out the trap outdoors with a hose.

Reverse the steps to replace the trap. Turn both collars at least two turns by hand to make sure the threads are matched up, then make them as tight as you can with the pipe wrench. An adult should do the final tightening job to make the joints as leak proof as possible. Run some water in the sink to check for leaks. If you see any drips, tighten the screw collars more, or remove the trap and replace the rubber seals before putting it back.

Backyard gym

ELECTIVE 18

Have you ever visited a gym or health club? You can build your own gym in your backyard. If you don't have room, don't give up. Your den can build a gym set to use in a pack outdoor fun day. Here are some ideas. You can find more in *Boys' Life* magazine and these two pamphlets: *Games for Cub Scouts* and *Cub Scout Activities*.

REQUIREMENTS

__a. **Build and use an outdoor gym with at least three items from this list.**

    (1) Balance board   **(5) Tetherball**

    (2) Trapeze   **(6) Climbing rope**

    (3) Tire walk   **(7) Running long**

    (4) Tire swing   **jump area**

__b. **Build three outdoor toss games.**

__c. **Plan an outdoor game or gym day with your den (this can be a part of a pack activity). Put your plans on paper.**

__d. **Hold an open house for your backyard gym.**

BANGBOARD CLOWN On any old plank or board, paint a large clown. Cut openings for the mouth and pockets. Make them different sizes. Toss your beanbag or ball through the openings.

CAN CATCHER Fasten large tin cans on a post. Put some straight up and some slanting up a little. Try tossing a ball into each one. Try it from different places. This helps improve your ability to judge distance.

BOX GOLF Set up nine cartons and number them. Throw your ball into No. 1. If you miss, throw from where you pick up your ball. When you've gotten it in No. 1, move to No. 2. Get someone to play with you.

BOX GOLF

TIRE WALK

TETHER BALL

BURY PIPE IN GROUND TO TAKE TETHER BALL POLE

Swimming

Swimming is a lot of fun!

When you learn to swim, you have a skill you can enjoy all your life. Whether you swim for fun or for sport, you can enjoy it winter or summer, and share the fun with your friends. (Remember, NEVER SWIM ALONE!)

REQUIREMENTS

__a. **Jump feetfirst into water over your head, swim 25 feet, turn around, and swim back.**

__b. **Swim on your back, using a resting stroke, for 30 feet.**

__c. **Rest by floating on your back, using as little motion as possible. Also show the "drown-proof" method of floating facedown for 4 minutes. ("Drown-proof" floating or bobbing [jellyfish float] uses a minimum of arm and leg movement to lift the head for breathing.)**

__d. **Tell what is meant by the buddy plan and the basic rules of safe swimming and simple rescue.**

__e. **Do a racing dive from edge of pool and swim 60 feet, using a racing stroke.**

There is something about this elective that is different from any other. That is this rule: Whenever you are working on Swimming, you must always have an adult with you who can swim.

NO.	DATE	ADULT SIGNATURE	✔ DEN CHART
19.			
19.			
19.			
19.			
19.			

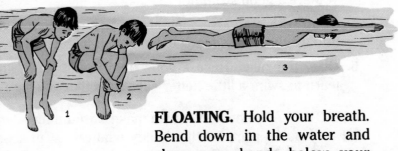

FLOATING. Hold your breath. Bend down in the water and clasp your hands below your knees. Presto, you'll float like a cork! Stretch out your arms and legs and you will still float.

BACK FLOAT. Stretch your arms to the side and lie back in the water, letting your feet float. Hold a deep breath. The water will just cover your ears. Relax, breathe normally. This is a good way to rest in the water.

ELECTIVE 19   227

BASIC RULES OF SAFE SWIMMING

1. Be physically fit.

2. Have a qualified adult present when you swim.

3. Swim in tested areas where there are no deep holes, stumps, rocks, cans, or glass.

4. If you can't swim, don't go in water over 3½ feet deep. If you can swim 50 feet, it's safe to go in water up to the top of your head. Go in deep water only if you are a good swimmer.

5. Swim with a buddy—someone to help you if you get into trouble, someone you can help if he needs it.

6. Obey the rules. Have a good time in the water and learn to swim a little better each time that you go in.

BUDDY PLAN. The buddy plan makes swimming safer.

Every boy is paired with a buddy who can swim about as well as he can. Buddies check in and out of the swimming area together.

All boys are checked in the water about every 10 minutes. The adult in charge signals for a buddy check with a single blast of a whistle or ring of a bell and a

call of "buddies!" He counts slowly to 10 while buddies join and raise hands and remain still and silent. Guards check all areas, count the pairs, and compare the total with the number known to be in the water. Two blasts or bells is the signal to resume swimming.

At the end of the swim, a final buddy check is made and every boy is accounted for. Three blasts or bells is the signal for immediate checkout.

SIDESTROKE. This is a good stroke to swim a long way because it is not very tiring.

Lie on your side in the water. Either side is OK. Your legs do what is called the scissors kick. Part them in the water as far as you can, and then bring them together as hard as you can.

At the same time, your arm which is lowest in the water reaches forward and pulls hard through the water toward your body. The top arm makes a shorter stroke as the bottom arm is coming back.

JUMP ENTRY. Jumping into the water feetfirst with legs and arms spread out and forward is a safe way to enter strange waters. Don't dive if you don't know what the pool is like. You could hurt your head or neck if the water is shallow or if there is a big rock near the surface.

If you are jumping from more than 4 feet above water, keep your feet together and your legs straight. Hold your nose with one hand as you jump.

RACING DIVE. In swimming races, you want to start fast and land in the water in a racing position. Stand with your feet slightly apart with the toes gripping the edge of the pool or dock. Crouch slightly with arms back, palms up.

On the signal, leap and swing your arms forward. You'll land in a swimming position.

RACING STROKE. This stroke is called the American crawl. It is for fast swims, but it can be tiring over long distances.

Start by floating face down with your arms and legs extended. Begin to kick fast and evenly. Try to keep your legs straight.

As you kick, reach one arm forward as far as it will go. Then pull it back hard through the water. When it gets about halfway back, reach forward with the other arm and stroke.

To take a breath, turn the head to one side out of the water as you stroke with the arm on the opposite side.

BACKSTROKE. Begin by floating on your back, arms down to your sides. Bring your hands up over your chest to your shoulders. Reach straight outward and a little beyond your head. Then pull your arms back hard to your sides. At the same time you are beginning the arm movement, draw your knees back like a frog, keeping your feet together. Then spread your legs wide to the sides (just as your arm pull begins) and snap them together to the starting position. Breathe in through your mouth just before each stroke.

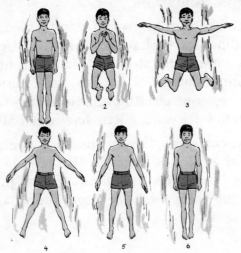

Sports

If you like sports, you aren't alone! Here are some more fun electives that will help you earn arrow points while you learn new sports skills.

REQUIREMENTS

__a. In archery, know the safety rules. Know how to shoot correctly. Put six arrows into a 4-foot target at a distance of 15 yards. Make an arrow holder.

__b. In skiing, know the Skier's Safety Code. Demonstrate walking and kick turn, climbing with sidestep or herringbone, snowplow stop, stem turn, four linked snowplow or stem turns, and straight running in a downhill position, or a cross-country position, and show how to recover from a fall.

__c. In ice skating, know the safety rules. From a standing start, skate forward 150 feet; come to a complete stop within 20 feet. Skate around a corner clockwise and counterclockwise without coasting. Show a turn from forward to backward. Skate backward 50 feet.

__d. In track, show how to make a sprint start. Run the 50-yard dash in 10 seconds or less. Show how to do the standing long jump, the running long jump, or high jump. Land in a soft area.

__e. **In roller skating, know the safety rules. From a standing start, skate forward 150 feet; come to a complete stop within 20 feet. Skate around a corner clockwise and counterclockwise without coasting and show a turn from forward to backward. Skate backward 50 feet.**

NO.	DATE	ADULT SIGNATURE	✓ DEN CHART
20.			
20.			
20.			
20.			
20.			

HOW TO SHOOT WITH BOW AND ARROW. Hold bow level and lay arrow across it, touching your forefinger. Nock arrow with cock feather turned up. Face target sideways. As you raise bow to straight-up shooting position, take aim and draw string back until hand touches chin. Keep your left arm stiff. Release arrow smoothly by opening string fingers quickly.

ARCHERY SAFETY RULES
- Never nock an arrow until ready to shoot.
- Never aim an arrow toward anyone.
- Shoot only where you have a clear view all around.

THE SKIER'S SAFETY CODE

- Ski only when properly equipped and clothed.
- Never ski alone.
- Ski under control, which means being able to turn and stop when you want.
- Ski only on slopes suited to your ability.
- Try to check trail before skiing down it.

SIDESTEP

HERRINGBONE

ICE SKATING SAFETY RULES

- Always use sharp skates.
- Skate only on approved ice surfaces.
- Never skate alone.
- Watch where you are skating at all times.
- Never throw anything on the ice.
- Never shove or grab another skater.

Four inches of new ice is safe for a crowd. Stay ashore until it is tested and approved for skating. Ice is unsafe after midwinter and spring thaws.

Springs bubbling up from lake or river bottoms will prevent water from freezing. Such openings in an ice field are known as "air holes." Streams, windswept lakes, tidal rivers, and salt water are slow to freeze and dangerous except after very cold weather.

Bushes, small trees, or danger signs should mark unsafe spots in daytime. Flares or lights should be used to mark them at night.

RIME AND REASON

1 INCH - KEEP OFF!

3 INCHES - SMALL GROUPS

2 INCHES - ONE MAY

4 INCHES - O.K.

ROLLER SKATING SAFETY RULES
FOR OUTDOOR SKATING

- Give pedestrians the right-of-way.

- Obey all laws about skating on the sidewalks or in the street.

- Don't race out of blind alleys and driveways.

- Avoid skating on chipped, broken, and rough areas. Watch out for rocks, branches, or trees.

- Don't skate on other people's sidewalks or driveways without their permission.

- Come to a complete stop and look in all directions for traffic before crossing streets.

- Obey traffic laws, signs, and signals.

- Don't skate in the street where traffic is heavy. If traffic is heavy, take off your skates and walk to a safe place.

- Avoid uncontrolled coasting and skating down inclines.

- Don't hitch onto bicycles, autos, or trucks.

- Don't skate outdoors at night.

- Check your equipment before skating. Tighten nuts and bolts. If using strap skates, keep straps dry and well oiled. Replace old straps when they are worn.

SPRINT START. Because sprints are short races, a sprinter must get a fast start and run at full speed all the way.

To make a fast start, a sprinter crouches low, and leans forward, with all fingers of both hands touching the ground at the starting line. One foot is far behind the other, with heels off the ground. At the signal, he shoves off hard with his rear foot and is at full stride right away.

LONG JUMPING. In the standing long jump, the jumper leaps as far as he can from the starting line into a sandpit. In the running long jump, he is allowed to make a run up to the line before leaping.

Both standing and running long jumpers try to fall forward rather than backward in landing.

HIGH JUMP. There are two styles of high jumping. In one, the jumper approaches the bar from the side and throws up first the leg nearest the bar and then the other in in a scissors kick.

In the other style, the jumper rolls over the bar by leaping and turning his whole body toward the bar. As he goes over, he is looking down at the bar.

Sales

The idea of selling something goes back a long way. People were trading things even before money was invented. When people traded, each one would give something for something else he wanted more. In a sale, everyone should feel better off than he or she was before the sale. Money is an easier way of keeping track of how much things are worth.

REQUIREMENTS

__a. **Take part in a pack-sponsored, money-earning sales program. Keep track of the sales you make yourself. When the sale is over, add up the sales you have sold.**

__b. **Help with a garage sale or rummage sale. This can be with your family, a neighbor, or a church, school, or pack event.**

NO.	DATE	ADULT SIGNATURE	✔ DEN CHART
21.			
21.			

ARROW POINT TRAIL

When you sell something (except tickets to a Scouting event), you should not wear your Cub Scout uniform. People should buy your product because they want it, not because you are a Cub Scout.

Collecting things

ELECTIVE **22**

Many people like to collect things as a hobby. Some things that are collected are stamps, coins, and emblems. Collections are just for fun, but you can't help but learn something about other places when you find a stamp, coin, or emblem from somewhere a long way from where you live.

REQUIREMENTS

__a. **Start a stamp collection. You can get information about stamp collecting at any U.S. Post Office.**

__b. **Mount and display a collection of emblems, coins, or other things to show at a pack meeting. This can be any kind of collection. Every time you show a different kind of collection, it counts as one requirement.**

NO.	DATE	ADULT SIGNATURE	✔ DEN CHART
22.			
22.			
22.			
22.			

ARROW POINT TRAIL

There are many ads in *Boys' Life* magazine for stamps and other things that can be collected. If an ad says that stamps will be sent "on approval," that means you either will have to pay for the stamps sent to you or mail them back. Some companies will give free stamps if you agree to let them send you others "on approval." You should not order these stamps unless you have enough money to buy them or pay the postage to mail them back.

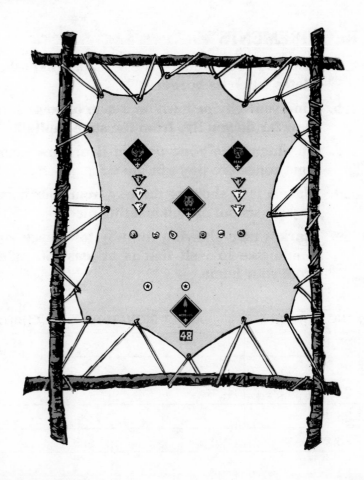

Maps

When explorers scout a new land, they make maps to show others what they find. Maps mean adventure, excitement, and imaginary trips. They are also useful for exploring your town and state.

REQUIREMENTS

__a. **Look up your state on a U.S. map. What other states touch its borders?**

__b. **Find your city or town on a map of your state. How far do you live from the state capital?**

__c. **In which time zone do you live? How many time zones are there in the U.S.?**

__d. **Make a map showing the way from your home to your school or den meeting place.**

__e. **Mark a map showing the way to a place you would like to visit that is at least 50 miles from your home.**

NO.	DATE	ADULT SIGNATURE	✓ DEN CHART
23.			
23.			
23.			
23.			
23.			

TES —	CAPITALS —
BAMA	MONTGOMERY
SKA	JUNEAU
ZONA	PHOENIX
ANSAS	LITTLE ROCK
FORNIA	SACRAMENTO
ORADO	DENVER
NECTICUT	HARTFORD
AWARE	DOVER
RIDA	TALLAHASSEE
RGIA	ATLANTA
VAII	HONOLULU
HO	BOISE
NOIS	SPRINGFIELD
ANA	INDIANAPOLIS
A	DES MOINES
NSAS	TOPEKA
TUCKY	FRANKFORT
ISIANA	BATON ROUGE
NE	AUGUSTA
RYLAND	ANNOPOLIS
SSACHUSETTS	BOSTON
HIGAN	LANSING
NNESOTA	ST. PAUL
SISSIPPI	JACKSON
SSOURI	JEFFERSON CITY
NTANA	HELENA
BRASKA	LINCOLN
VADA	CARSON CITY
N HAMPSHIRE	CONCORD
N JERSEY	TRENTON
N MEXICO	SANTE FE
N YORK	ALBANY
RTH CAROLINA	RALEIGH
RTH DAKOTA	BISMARCK
HO	COLUMBUS
LAHOMA	OKLAHOMA CITY
EGON	SALEM
NNSYLVANIA	HARRISBURG
ODE ISLAND	PROVIDENCE
UTH CAROLINA	COLUMBIA
UTH DAKOTA	PIERRE
NNESSEE	NASHVILLE
XAS	AUSTIN
AH	SALT LAKE CITY
RMONT	MONTPELIER
RGINIA	RICHMOND
ASHINGTON	OLYMPIA
ST VIRGINIA	CHARLESTON
SCONSIN	MADISON
OMING	CHEYENNE

ELECTIVE 23

Indian life

Indians were already in America when Columbus got here. They tell many stories about where they came from, but nobody knows for sure. They hunted for their food and also grew plants that people in the rest of the world did not have. Indians gave us corn, squash, and pumpkins. They lived close to nature and had their own laws and religions.

REQUIREMENTS

__a.   Indians lived all over what is now the United States. Find the name of the tribe who lived nearest where you live now. What is this tribe best known for?

__b.   Make and display a sand painting.

__c.   Learn, make equipment for, and play two Indian games with members of your den. Be able to tell the rules, who won, and what the score was.

__d.   Make a model of an Indian house.

NO.	DATE	ADULT SIGNATURE	✔ DEN CHART
24.			
24.			
24.			
24.			

RAINBOW BOY AND CORN PEOPLE

RED BLUE BLACK WHITE TAN BACKGROUND BLUE YELLOW

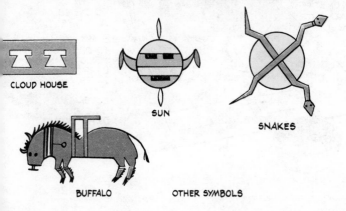

CLOUD HOUSE

SUN

SNAKES

BUFFALO

OTHER SYMBOLS

SAND PAINTINGS are made by Navaho medicine men. They are made in one night, then destroyed. Navahos believe it is bad luck to let the sun rise on a sand painting. Of course you will want to keep yours, so here is one way to make a sand painting you can hang on the wall.

Navahos make their sand paintings on the clean sand floor of the hogan, or hut. They use five colors: black,

ELECTIVE 24

white, blue-gray, yellow and red, and make the patterns by sifting sand through their fingers. The finished sand paintings are used in religious ceremonies.

You will need fine white sand for this; ordinary brown beach sand does not take the color well. Mix 4 cups of sand with 1½ tablespoons of *dry* tempera paint (from art supply store.) Mix well. Add more tempera for darker colors and more sand for lighter colors. Store in margarine tubs or paper cups.

③ SPRINKLE COLORED SAND ON WET GLUE.

① DRAW OR TRACE PATTERN ON STIFF PAPER OR LIGHT CARDBOARD

② PAINT PATTERN WITH THINNED WHITE GLUE

DO ONE COLOR AT A TIME

START WITH LIGHT COLORS (WHITE, TAN, YELLOW,) AND DO DARKER COLORS LATER

COVER SMALL AREAS SO GLUE WON'T DRY TOO FAST.

④ POUR OFF EXTRA SAND.

INDIAN GAMES helped make young Braves quick of hand and sharp of eye, very useful skills for future hunters. Try your hand at these.

MOTOWU is played with feathered darts made from corncobs. When you have corn-on-the-cob, save the cobs and dry them. Cut them all to the same length, about

3½ to 4 inches, and smooth them with a piece of coarse sandpaper glued to a wood block. Make holes at both ends. Using white glue, glue a 2½-inch stick or dowel in the smaller end and two turkey feathers in the big end. You will need at least four darts.

MOTOWU

Play this game like you do horseshoes. Place two flower pots or baskets about 10 inches in diameter 12 to 15 feet apart. Each player takes turns, throwing two darts at the same time. Darts are held in the same hand with the index finger between them. You can throw directly at the basket, or toss them up in the air, which makes them spin. Both darts must go into the basket; first player to get two darts in at the same time wins the game. This is a game played by the Hopi Indians in Arizona.

Indians from Zuni Pueblo play **POKEAN.** They make a kind of shuttlecock from corn husks and feathers. Save the husks from corn-on-the-cob and dry them. Don't let them dry until they are brittle, but make your pokean while they are still soft enough to bend. You will need three corn husks 1½ inches wide and 6 or 7 inches long, and a fourth piece about ¾ inch wide and 5 inches long. Take one of the three large pieces and fold it in thirds, to make a pad. Lay the other two big pieces on a flat surface to make a cross. Put the pad in the center. Fold the bottom husk over the top husk and pad. Then bring the ends at the top together over the center. Don't twist. Wrap the ends with the small strip. Wrap a string snugly two or three times around the ends and tie. Glue three feathers into the top with white glue. They will make the pokean twirl in the air.

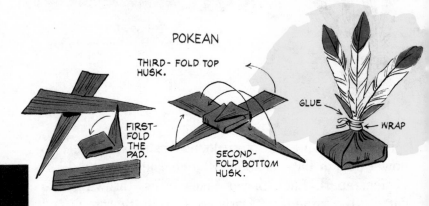

POKEAN

THIRD-FOLD TOP HUSK.

FIRST-FOLD THE PAD.

SECOND-FOLD BOTTOM HUSK.

GLUE

WRAP

Each player tries to keep his pokean in the air by hitting it with his hand. The object of the game is to count the number of times you can hit it to keep it in the air before it falls. The player with the highest score wins the game.

INDIAN HOUSES were built to suit the kind of area of America where they lived. Tribes who lived on the plains built portable buffalo skin tents called *teepees*. In the wet northwest they built wood houses with sloping roofs. In the Southwest they built stone houses under overhanging cliffs. Navahos live where wood is scarce. They use short logs to build many-sided houses they call *hogans*. In the far north, they built houses out of snow blocks. Indians learned to live wherever they happened to be.

HOGAN

PUEBLO

IGLOO

SEMINOLE PIT HOUSE

WIGWAM

TEPEE

WICKIUP

Get Set for
WEBELOS

When you are 10 years old or have completed the fourth grade, you can join a Webelos den and wear the yellow, green, and red Webelos colors.

There will be 15 activity badges that you can wear on the colors. Do you like science? You can win the activity badges for Geologist, Scientist, and Naturalist.

Perhaps you like the outdoor life. Well, you'll find activity area badges for Outdoorsman, Sportsman, Athlete, Forester, and Aquanaut.

There's much more. As a Webelos Scout, you also can wear the Craftsman, Engineer, Traveler, Citizen, Artist, Showman. and Scholar badges.

There are two reasons for all these activities. One is to offer you more fun. The other is to prepare you to be a Boy Scout. As a matter of fact in some packs you may be able to wear the Khaki uniform when you become a Webelos.

When you are 10½ or older and have completed the fifth grade, you can become a Boy Scout. You'll be ready to do that if you join the Webelos den and take part in the activities.

To welcome you into the the Webelos den, your Cubmaster probably will have a special ceremony at a pack meeting. You will be given the Webelos badge colors. When you get home, ask your mother to take off your old den numeral and to pin the Webelos badge colors on your right sleeve.

Sew your old den numeral on your red patch vest, if you have one.

See page 256.

BIG BEAR TRAIL RECORD

		Do	of these
		▼	▼

Do one for GOD

☐ 1. Ways We Worship   1   a

☐ 2. Emblems of Faith   1   a

Do three for COUNTRY

☐ 3. What Makes America Special?   4   a b c d e f g

☐ 4. Tall Tales   3   a b c

☐ 5. Sharing Your World With Wildlife   4   a b c d e

☐ 6. Take Care of Your Planet   3   a b c d e f

☐ 7. Law Enforcement Is a Big Job   4   a b c d e f g

Do four for FAMILY

☐ 8. The Past Is Exciting and Important   3   a b c d e f

☐ 9. What's Cooking?   4   a b c d e f

☐ 10. Family Fun   2   a b

☐ 11. Be Ready!   4   a b c d e

☐ 12. Family Outdoor Adventures   3   a b c d e

☐ 13. Saving Well, Spending Well   4   a b c d e f g

Do four for SELF

☐ 14. Ride Right!   4   a b c d e f g

☐ 15. Games, Games, Games   2   a b c

☐ 16. Building Muscles   3   a b c

☐ 17. Information Please   4   a b c d e f

☐ 18. Jot It Down   5   a b c d e f g

☐ 19. Shavings and Chips   4   a b c d

☐ 20. Sawdust and Nails   3   a b c

☐ 21. Build a Model   3   a b c d e f

☐ 22. Tying It All Up   5   a b c d e f

☐ 23. Sports, Sports, Sports   5   a b c d e

☐ 24. Be a Leader   3   a b c d e

▲

Circle the ones you do.

Then make an X on the ones you use for arrow point credit

like this: 3 ⓐⓑⓒ d ⊗ ▶

ARROW POINT TRAIL

ARROW POINT TRAIL RECORD

Achievement Number and Letter	Elective Number and Letter	Elective Number and Letter
24e		

How to Wear
Cub Scout
INSIGNIA

DIRECTIONS FOR PARENTS. The actual-size diagrams on the inside front and back covers of this book will show you the sizes, shapes, location, and method of attaching the insignia your son will be eligible to wear as a Cub Scout.

SLEEVE INSIGNIA. Use the diagram on the page as a guide for sleeve insignia. (a) Center the edge of the page on the crease of the sleeve, (b) line up shoulder seams of page and shirt, (c) mark exact location of the badge with white chalk, (d) pin to sleeve.

All Cub Scouts, regardless of rank, wear the sleeve insignia indicated. Remove old insignia before attaching new. Your son will wear only the appropriate insignia of the position he holds.

POCKET INSIGNIA. When your son wins the Bear badge, he wears it centered on the left side of the left pocket, in line with the pocket flap. (See inside front cover.) When he earns a Gold Arrow Point, it goes ¾ inch below the Bear badge. Silver Arrow Points go directly below the gold. The size of your son's shirt pocket depends upon his shirt size, but you will find that his Bobcat, Wolf, and Bear badges will fit easily on the average-size pocket as shown. He wears the Immediate Recognition Award on the right pocket.

TO SEW. Following the instructions on these pages, locate the exact position of the insignia, check with a ruler, if necessary, and pin or baste to the shirt. Use a fine overhand, back, blind, or buttonhole stitch to sew on the insignia. Thread should match the border of the emblem. When using a sewing machine, follow manufacturer's instructions for stitching badges and emblems.

PARENT GUIDE